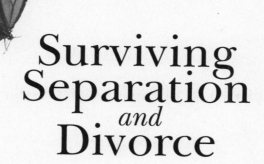

Surviving Separation *and* Divorce

Other Books by Loriann Hoff Oberlin

Writing For Money

Working at Home While the Kids Are There, Too

The Insider's Guide To Pittsburgh

The Angry Child
(co-author with Timothy F. Murphy, Ph.D.)

Surviving Separation *and* Divorce

A Woman's Guide to Making It Through the First Year

Loriann Hoff Oberlin

Adams Media Corporation
Holbrook, Massachusetts

Published by
Adams Media Corporation
260 Center Street, Holbrook, MA 02343. U.S.A.
www.adamsmedia.com

ISBN: 1-58062-303-4

Printed in Canada.

J I H G F E D C

Library of Congress Cataloging-in-Publication Data
Hoff Oberlin, Loriann.
Surviving separation and divorce / Loriann Hoff Oberlin.
p. cm.
Includes bibliographical references and index.
ISBN 1-58062-303-4
1. Divorce—Case studies. 2. Separation (Psychology)—Case studies. I. Title.
HQ814 .H67 2000
306.89—dc21
99-059250

This publication is designed to provide accurate and authoritative information with regard to the subject matter covered. It is sold with the understanding that the publisher is not engaged in rendering legal, accounting, or other professional advice. If legal advice or other expert assistance is required, the services of a competent professional person should be sought.

—From a *Declaration of Principles* jointly adopted by a Committee of the American Bar Association and a Committee of Publishers and Associations

DISCLAIMER

This book is intended to provide accurate information for women facing a marital separation, but is sold with the understanding that neither the publisher nor the author is engaged in rendering any financial, investment, legal, tax, or other advice. If you desire specific advice, consult a trusted and competent professional.

In order to protect the privacy of individuals who generously shared life experiences and thoughts for this research, only professional experts are quoted by name and identifying factors. All other names and identifying circumstances have been altered to protect their identity. In some instances, composites of two or three persons have been used to obscure them and to clarify the relevant issues. Any similarities between the anecdotes the author presents and any actual person, living or deceased, is entirely coincidental.

Michael W. Smith sings a song dedicated to friends, and his words inspire me to dedicate this book to my friends who saw me through a difficult time. They believed in me, and I believe in them. Friends are friends forever, and I have some of the best!

Contents

Acknowledgments

Surviving a separation teaches you to call in all the supports, and did I ever! There are simply too many people to list here who were instrumental as I gained back my confidence, courage, and energy to make a new life for myself and my children. They know who they are—family, friends, and neighbors, ministers, doctors, and lawyers—their encouragement sustained me, and still does.

My children need to be thanked, for they asked for none of this. Andy and Alex, I love you more than anything in this world, and your courage and ability to adapt have amazed me. You are great kids!

My dear friend Donna Israel gave important feedback and encouraged me to pursue a book proposal on this subject. Pam Liflander at Adams was the first editor I sent it to, and I thank her for recognizing the passion I had for this project.

Those who contributed their professional expertise include Kevin Deem; Mary O'Brien, M.D.; Timothy F. Murphy, Ph.D.; and Karen Myers of the Payne Myers law practice in Pittsburgh. Additionally, my thanks to everyone at the Women's Center & Shelter of Greater Pittsburgh as well as members of the East Suburban Task Force Against Domestic Abuse/Violence for the knowledge they have imparted to me.

Finally, my sincere appreciation goes out to the many women who freely shared their personal stories, tips, humorous anecdotes, and general advice for the benefit of my readers. You've helped to make this a true resource with a breadth of views for those who need it most.

Introduction

Back in 1995, upon the release of my first book, our metropolitan paper featured my profile in its Saturday section. The Dossier column was pretty popular, and I was excited not only for the book's publicity, but because I would surprise my husband, who never missed reading this column. My greatest accomplishment I'd listed for all to read was the work I'd put into my marriage, along with raising my two sons. And whom would I most want to have dinner with? Besides Fred Rogers and Hillary Clinton, I listed my husband.

Well, within two weeks, Fred and Hillary were still on my list. There were things I could have done with my husband, but having dinner with him wasn't first in mind! Eight days after that public pronouncement of my devotion to him, I learned things that shattered my idea of a happy marriage.

If you're like me, you'll never forget the precise moment you realized your marriage was pretty much over, at least in the sense you knew it. Close friends remember the date. I called one at 5 AM, having failed to cry myself to sleep that night. My doctor remembers the crisis, for I ran to her with my fears, and my poor minister found me in his office, his first day back from summer vacation.

Looking back, I know I wouldn't have survived without the compassion these people showed me. I thought the world was coming to an end. In a sense, my world had already hit a meteor, and its pieces were spinning out of control.

Imagine feeling shocked, numb, as if you're in an abyss. I felt lost wondering if I would fit in anywhere. I was surely puzzled. Enter the "what if" stage when one's mind tends to ruminate with "what if I'd done this, said that?" Of course, I also felt terribly alone. If home is where the heart is supposed to be, the separated woman soon finds it the very source of her hurt and anguish. You feel used, with promises broken, dreams blown away. And finally, I know I felt a bit helpless, for it seemed I could do nothing to change this reality.

Though time has passed, I can still feel some of the heartache. Events took their toll, and weeks later, my husband walked out, having insisted to me, and to friends and family, that he wanted a separation. Today, we're divorced. On one hand that's a fortunate outcome; on another, it's simply tragic. The pain was sharp, my hurt very real and justified, and the questions of "why" never satisfactorily answered. Above everything, my children lost their family. Forever. No child wants nor deserves this.

In better times I would have welcomed dinner with my husband. We were college sweethearts and had a chapel wedding. We survived his graduate schooling, built our dream house in the suburbs, began our family, and even endured the frightening birth of our second son three months premature. That summer, as we confronted some tough issues, we faced a corporate transfer, a move that might have brought us closer and yielded additional opportunities for us both. Indeed, we could have had a bright future together.

The positive aspect of the breakup is that throughout the first few weeks and months of our separation, I started to breathe freely again. While it took me many months to seek counseling at a women's shelter for my sons and myself, not having to feel threatened and live with household rage was wonderful. I came to understand what others have described as crazymaking behavior, when you're so confused because you've allowed others to define your reality that you don't even know what balance and stability mean.

In my situation, since additional issues of trust had been trampled, I learned to rely upon friends—great friends—the kind you can call in the middle of the night with your worst nightmare. Equally, I learned to trust in myself. Despite wanting to believe in the "it'll never happen again" phase many wives endure, I sought legal advice in those early weeks that served me well.

Listening to others' impressions really lifted me out of the abyss I felt trapped in. Friends and outsiders I trusted could view things more objectively, and soon I began to see more wrong than right with my marriage. Holding it together became more work than it was worth, even for the sake of my children, who were increasingly affected.

I sensed clear signals, for six steady weeks at least, that my husband wasn't in the marriage. Yes, I was at first in deep denial. My realization or wake-up call came about more gradually so that by the night he drove away, I wasn't quite as stunned. And as it became overwhelmingly clear to me that circumstances weren't changing, I altered course. I got stronger, taking legal and safety measures that were necessary, albeit difficult.

That's why you're reading this book. I know first hand the struggle involved in starting over, doing an about-face at the worst possible time, when you're emotionally drained, perhaps physically weak from stress, poor diet, and fatigue, and when you still must get up to work each day and raise your children. This book will show you how it's done, in incremental steps. It will help you summon your own inner strength and resolve to make life better for you, and your children. It will urge you ahead, not backwards.

Of course, that forward direction might mean a reconciliation. It's indeed possible, and perhaps your best outcome. We'll discuss reconciliation in a later chapter. For those who haven't officially separated yet and are mulling it over, these discussions may very well influence your decision.

But, if like many women, you held out hope and patience long enough, and especially if a separation has been forced upon you, you'll realize that you can indeed survive this and any ensuing divorce.

Divorce is difficult, and this book will prepare you for that legal journey. Yet this is *not* a book about how to obtain the best settlement, how to take your man for everything he's worth, or how to understand each state's legal intricacies. There are plenty of those already. In fact, I spend a good bit of time discussing the weeks, months, even years of separation because too few resources do that.

This book is about you, your life, your emotional, physical, social, and spiritual well-being. From how to safeguard your health, your property, and your personal safety (and sanity!) to how to maintain your career and finances, your family unit, heck, even your lawn, this book is for you. It's a lifestyle book, not a legal tome.

So take the time—no make the time—to focus on you and your world without a moment's guilt. You're dealing with a lot right now, and you deserve some time to regroup. While this escape might not rank up there with a romance novel (and I doubt you're in the mood for a bodice-ripper right now!), turn these pages with pride that you are taking an all-important step toward recovery and some sort of resolution of your marital crisis.

In the pages ahead, you'll learn from several perspectives, including experts in the fields of health care, personal finance, law, home security, child development, psychology, and women's advocacy. I'll share the experiences of other women who have traveled this painful journey and survived.

I'm proud to say in the years since separation hit me that I'm a much more confident person with the ability to look ahead more than behind. Friends tell me I take charge of situations more easily, I laugh more, and that I've weathered this well. In myself, I do see more of a can-do attitude, and I've learned that I'm attractive, vibrant, and sought after. Let me tell you, there *are* kind, considerate, and mature men out there who bring a smile to your face. Most of all, there is indeed life after anguish. You'll find it, just as I did, only with patience and a little time.

—Loriann Hoff Oberlin

Chapter One

Suddenly Separated

The day you realize you're being left, or that you need to leave, is a span of hours filled with mixed emotions that often pierce like shrapnel. If you're leaving, you may feel guilty and question your decision. If you're the one left behind, you might be thrust into a pattern of crazymaking, or you might find you're just coming out of one.

When I say crazymaking, I mean a feeling of being off balance, a little lost (or a lot), with a muddled mind and maybe even broken promises. If you feel that your husband is defining your reality to the point that you're bewildered and you feel increasingly inadequate, then you might be experiencing what experts call crazymaking.

When the true reality sinks in, the prevailing emotion is shock. How could this happen? How could he do this? Shock is followed by fear, anger, concern for the children. It's an emotional roller coaster. Soon, the very real tasks laid before you require your focus and attention. But right when it's time for action, you'd rather sink into a hole and never come out again.

Realize as you read this book that you're not alone. Plenty of other women have traveled this unpleasant journey, and the good news is, they are living better lives. Hold on to that hope. You have a lot to look forward to, and once you face the unpleasant events, there are wonderful times to come.

When the Bottom Falls Out

When I got the clear message from my own husband not to wait up at night, and that he wanted an apartment of his own, one of my witty friends exclaimed, "What does he want to do, go order pizza with his own toppings for a month?"

Whether it's pizza or some other pleasure, there are lessons every woman can learn. Don't feel weak that you need to regroup and do some remedial work reminiscent of "Emotions 101." You didn't expect this passage. Especially at this important juncture, the actions you take and the mistakes you make will most decidedly matter.

If you don't feel up to making decisions on that first or second day after the news hits you, or when you realize you must initiate a separation yourself, allow yourself some quiet time. Taking time to reflect, to pray, to think, or simply to talk through your turmoil is far better than racing into inappropriate action you will regret later. Your strength will come.

In the immediate aftermath, your mind will race with thoughts, feelings, even pressures—some internal, some very real, and some placed upon you by well-meaning but clueless friends and family. Much of what follows may sound familiar.

How Could He?

The first question you'll often hear when a husband walks out is "How could he?" I hate to be the bearer of bad news, but you may never have an answer to that. Rest assured, you'll hear it again and again.

For you, it might be easier to slide the question aside each time it's uttered. But for me, the journalist always in search of answers, it was a real struggle not having any clear explanation. I coped by allowing myself time to gain perspective, to see things more clearly.

I reminded myself that I loved my husband with all my heart and soul, body and mind. There were times I showed this emotion beyond all doubt, and there were times I probably could have done a better job. I'm sure I could have been a better partner in some respects. Yet my conscience is clear. I held out hope and stood by my mate when other women might have bolted.

Looking back, it seemed that I spent so much time during my marriage trying to keep it together only to discover it wasn't worth the mental energy. I really had been the partner devoting most of the energy and making things happen in the marriage. In time, I realized how stubborn I had originally been. Good friends told me later that what I perceived as persistence in keeping the marriage going was coming off to them more like "how much more garbage is she going to take?"

There's no doubt I did the right thing being so persistent. I had two children with special needs. Above all, I did love this man, despite the pain.

As the weeks passed after our initial separation, I knew my friends were right. I could let go of the "how could he?"

because I could live with the outcome. If you have put substantial effort into seeking solutions and standing by your mate but it has not yielded positive results, try letting go as well. Shift the focus from "how could he?" to what comes next. What does come after this juncture? A new beginning—for you.

You'll Be Better Off

The morning after my husband walked out, my minister paid a visit. There I was with my box of tissues. I don't even remember if I offered the man a cup of coffee! But something he said—actually several things—made such complete sense that they gave me the peace my heart and my household desperately needed. "I think this separation needs to happen," was one bit of wisdom that I held on to that day.

Several other friends and family members reiterated the same, suggesting I would be much better off. Reluctantly, and slowly, that message sank in.

Many women will tell you that their husbands did them the favor of their lives by leaving them, or by forcing issues so that these women made the ultimate break. Go ahead and sigh at me. If you're not ready to accept that line, I understand. Right now, where you sit, just getting through the next hour might be a monumental task. You may not believe you can make a move without your husband. The longer you've been married, the more firmly planted that belief might be.

Some women—those who have initiated a breakup—also need to realize their new future. Even though they've made an important decision to exit, they will often have mixed emotions. We women are conditioned to be caretakers, and when something in our grasp fails, we feel responsible, as if there's still something else we could do to make it right. Essentially, all women facing a marital separation need to hear that they will be better off. A separation will cause clarity. One way or another, you will have resolution, in the form of reconciliation, or freedom.

Sink into Your Support System

The other side of that caretaker phenomenon is that we women are wonderful at taking care of each other. How is it that when we haven't slept, have lost our breakfast, and can't even get the words out right, our female friends know precisely what we need? What's more, they're quickly on the scene.

I remember the constant telephone support. It was my lifeline, in some respects a sanity check, particularly with one friend I must have spoken with almost every day for those first few months.

Having the hindsight of several years now, I can imagine how tedious it must have been to my best friends to continue the reassurance, the reiteration of such lines like "you did the right thing" or "you'll get through this." And high on my list of memories is the pan of lasagna that friends brought one evening. This couple had brought dinner to me as a new mom two years before, and we laughed to note that whenever a family member arrived or exited, the simple comfort of Italian cuisine, and my friend's culinary talents, went a long way toward healing!

Hopefully, this type of support is available to you as well. Friends can be amazingly creative when it comes to comfort, and I'm not just referring to the tangible surprises like lasagna, a box of chocolates, or a tall bottle of bubble bath. I'm talking about calls to check in on you, a shoulder to lean on, arms to hug you when it feels like you'll never again have close contact. These gifts don't cost anything but our friend's time, and they are given freely out of concern and love.

That should say something else to you in your most desperate moments. Friends wouldn't be expending the effort if they didn't feel you were worth it. And if you're like me, you'll often feel you've used up so many methods of support that your IOU list runneth over. Look at it this way. Life is never without its struggles for any one of us. In time, you will most surely be able to be there for friends who need a little payback. What you give really does come back to you, and vice versa.

For those women who are facing this marital crisis without family near or friends to lend a tangible hand, seek out the supports that are available. Call the office of your house of worship and schedule a time to talk with someone. If there has been abuse of any kind—emotional, physical, financial, sexual—contact your women's shelter and counseling agency. It's most likely listed in the phone book under county resources or nonprofit organizations. (See appendix for listings.)

Many cities have 24-hour hotline services for anyone going through a crisis. Trained counselors will reach out to you and are often armed with the right words to validate your feelings. They can also provide appropriate information and telephone numbers to contact. Of course, your own physician can be a great support and may often refer you to mental health therapists, social workers, or other counselors to help alleviate the burdens you face.

Take One Day at a Time

Who you are today is not who you will be tomorrow, next month, or certainly a year from now. The fears you have will be resolved, in one way or another. The days, with their individual tasks, will come, and they will pass. And when this happens, you'll feel growth and accomplishment.

That's largely how separation is, but convincing yourself of this when you desire answers right now is another matter. Of course, every woman's situation is unique. For the woman facing domestic violence, safety decisions are paramount and need to be addressed immediately. Those women left with little or no financial resources need to file for support as soon as possible in order to set a hearing date to settle the matter.

Your circumstances will dictate what deserves immediate attention, and what can wait. As a general rule, your agenda should involve drawing up a safety plan by changing locks or protecting yourself and your property; filing for child and spousal support (which you can do before you even engage an attorney); obtaining medical care if your health has been jeopardized; and caring for the emotional and tangible needs of your children. Much of the material presented in later chapters goes into greater detail in each of these areas.

If you're having trouble coping or even thinking about what comes first, ask a trusted friend or counselor to help you devise daily goals and a to-do list. An objective party who is not emotionally caught up in the crisis can see things more clearly, more quickly. Just remember not to overwhelm yourself with too many extraneous details that could be handled in the weeks and months to come.

Halt Hasty Decisions

When my separation began, I had known others who had been separated so I was fairly familiar with Pennsylvania law. I knew, for instance, that there was a two-year waiting period that one party could invoke to halt any hasty decisions.

Honestly, it took me the first few weeks to gather my thoughts and feelings. I needed to listen to my support system instead of my estranged husband. While in anger, it would have been easy to declare "I'm out of this marriage" or "I'm filing for divorce tomorrow." Instead, I'm glad I waited.

Often, quick decisions aren't appropriate decisions. Some distance between the parties might clarify some matters, making reconciliation possible. A hasty judgment to divorce today might make it all but impossible to get back together tomorrow. In addition, if you earn less than your spouse, there might be financial reasons for you to take your time, particularly if there are children involved.

If you haven't separated yet and are reading this book, a word of caution. States vary in their laws regarding separation and divorce. Should your spouse want to move you both to another state, examine the laws closely as they apply to property division, alimony, and child support. It could be that he's seeking a sweeter deal in another land.

Each state varies in the amount of time a couple must live apart before a divorce can move forward. Since my youngest son had just turned two years old when my separation began, I was very concerned about his welfare. Ever since his premature birth, it had been necessary for me to be home with him to prevent illness and facilitate frequent therapy he required. A snap decision to divorce might have disrupted all that he needed, and all the supports I had in place. I knew that I had two years in which I could stay in our residence, receive child and spousal support, and have our medical insurance covered. For me, this grace period proved helpful. For other women, circumstances might be different. Just be sure that you don't make important legal decisions too quickly. Sometimes you can't revoke those choices, and you'll suffer unfortunate consequences for your hasty actions.

Waiting also provides a second scenario. You might be tempted to take your spouse back too soon. Reconciliation is certainly a potential outcome, and I don't want to detract from that possibility. However, I do know of many married men who dished a proverbial pile of garbage on their wives and then wondered why these women didn't beg their men to come back. The answer is they'd had enough. They got stronger. They grew. Their husbands didn't.

There is nothing wrong with fighting for your marriage. Just realize that some men will sit back and wait for the ego boost when their wives plead and cajole them back into the marriage. Read this book first, and just maybe you'll discover strength you never dreamed you had.

Avoid Other Actions

When you're most vulnerable, you'll feel a roller coaster of emotions. Some women use this time to get a better grasp on life, while others can't contain their own anger. These are powerful emotions and you have a right to them.

But I remember reading an advice column where a troubled teenage girl wrote in about her father who had left the family in an affair, and her mother who instantly sought the company of other men in an attempt to retaliate or replace her estranged husband. The girl was clearly ignored by two parents seeking a second adolescence. It sounded very troubling.

Some women retaliate by seeking the company of men too soon. One woman with young children lacked professional patience, getting a full-time job and putting her kids in daycare. She ultimately drove herself and her children crazy by the new routine. If you act hastily and get a full-time job too soon, you might jeopardize your chance of alimony. And if you have many men in your life, well, this could be used against you also.

Family Fallout

After the reality of a separation sets in, it's often painful to witness the same shock on the faces and in the voices of family members. There are women who hesitate divulging such information, for fear they will be chastised.

In some families when a daughter marries, parents see her husband as a new son. It's quite conceivable, especially in cases of abuse, that she hid from both families the pain she endured in the marriage. In cases like these, some families urge wives to try harder, overlook things, or otherwise downplay the realities she's lived with.

No one wants to believe that a son or son-in-law could be a batterer, a cheat, a drunk, an addict, or even a john. Most family members, especially those who haven't been brought along slowly and introduced to the reality of your struggles, will be shocked. When they learn about the separation and the reasons behind it, they may turn to denial: "That can't be" or

"I don't believe you." They may even blame you, asking, "What did you do to him?" These accusations could come from either family—most likely from his. Brace yourself for this type of reaction. Even if your parents, siblings, or in-laws promised to be there for you, there were probably qualifications on that promise.

Nothing you can do will make them magically face something they're not ready to face, to "get" an issue they aren't capable of grasping. Many times, your in-laws will dump even more complaints or criticisms on you to the extent that you feel like the family scapegoat. What matters most is what *you* think.

I still remember when one member in a family was faced with an unexpected divorce. The husband had left for another woman, and everyone questioned aloud how a man could act with such disregard for his family and the life he'd achieved. These typically tightlipped people made it emphatically clear: Didn't he realize that people would talk? Did this man think he could get away with this behavior? Years later, one of those who chastised did the same, or worse, to his own wife and children. Go figure!

I think if my own boys casually walked away from their families, behaved immorally, or committed a crime, that I wouldn't shift my standards. I'd remain true to my beliefs. I know firsthand how troubling it is when there is a double standard applied. The same family member who belittled someone else's husband for bolting out the door might have a sudden memory lapse or shift of opinion when it's convenient. Why? Because of the old expression about blood being thicker than water. Worse yet, some families simply lack a value system that guides any element of their lives, including their actions.

Yes, what matters most is what *you* think, and if you surround yourself with the right support people, you'll triumph. You won't have to worry if others, family members in particular, get it. Actually, for your own sanity's sake, it's probably helpful to assume they'll never understand your side of the story. Accept this and move on.

How to Help Your Separated Friend

Just in case your support system has rallied around, yet you're too confused to consider what you need, here's a handy list to share with those who truly care. Each woman's situation is different, but the following ideas should help most friends and families help those who are suddenly separated:

- Listen, but don't push your own agenda. Unless you feel your friend is making a grave mistake that will jeopardize her safety, finances, or legal standing, keep quiet and merely lend an ear. Be available for telephone chats at most any hour. Have patience, for you may hear the same ruminations, regrets, or fears until your friend works them through.
- Offer kind gestures without being asked. If your kids and hers play well together, schedule play dates. Treat them to a movie or park outing when you know their mother has so much on her mind she can't even think of entertaining her children. Drop off a cheer-up gift of bubble bath and tea. Even a home-cooked meal says you care.

- Provide companionship. Particularly if she's the only adult in the house, your friend will get lonely. Holidays and birthdays are hard that first year. Having a friend takes the oneness out of them. If you fear she's sitting home alone, invite her to a movie or over to chat on your couch.
- Call daily just to say hi and let her know you're concerned. Also, sending an occasional card to lighten the day sure beats nasty legal letters and bills.
- Help with objectivity, as best you can. When overwhelmed, none of us is qualified to make too many important decisions all at once. Be a sounding board for practical matters, and always keep your discussions confidential.
- Accompany your friend to court, a doctor's appointment, a women's shelter, or anywhere else you know she needs to go but is upset about.
- Ease her financial burdens by sharing. Offer clothing your children have outgrown. Provide baby-sitting so she can save the expense. Share the harvest of your garden when it yields more vegetables than you can consume. If you can afford it, buy a book or magazine you know would encourage her. Little things like these add up, and presented as friendly gestures, they won't affect her pride.
- Reassure her that this too shall pass. Reiterate that her marriage is only one aspect of her life that continues no matter what. Encourage her to take care of her own needs with good exercise, diet, and health care.

- Intervene if her condition worsens. Call her doctor or therapist if there is talk of suicide or alert other friends to check in on her too, once in a while.

The Truth Be Told . . . or Not?

Knowing when to let family ties go is vital when you encounter a separation. Knowing when to speak up and how to respond to questions from friends and family is equally pivotal.

One school of thought is to say nothing, to silence all negative thoughts out of respect for privacy and reputation. I'm more inclined to think that you do need to confide in someone you trust, whether it be a friend or counselor. In the first few hours when my marriage faced a real crisis, I remember a friend advising me, "Just be careful who you tell because once you say something, you can never take it back." That was wise advice.

For the first few weeks, I confided in only those people who needed to know or who could render assistance. I kept the stiff upper lip and maintained the facade that our marriage was still working. But as time passed, I recognized that there was little point to maintaining the status quo.

If I were an actress, I think I'd be dirt poor. I couldn't hide my emotions and I couldn't pretend there were four of us in a house when there were only three. I also didn't want to wonder who knew what, trying to be open with some, yet closed with others. Thus, in one-on-one dialogue, I shared my feelings with people quite openly.

Honesty of what transpired was the route I chose, partially to end my enabling, partially to preserve my own sanity. It might not be a path you feel comfortable with, given your emotions or your personality. Do what is best for you.

Be Yourself

Similar advice is to be yourself. But even that is difficult to follow if you have endured years of a miserable marriage, emotional battering, and perhaps depression. It's hard to get in touch with your true feelings when you're living a fantasy for everyone else's benefit.

Truly, one of the perks of a trial or even long-term separation is finding out things about yourself, and more important, focusing on your needs. With the wife role sidelined, you can concentrate on your children's needs and on your own interests. It's amazing how much time wives really do devote to their husbands, to making their partner's lives easier or more satisfying instead of their own.

One woman's true sense of humor shined when the husband was no longer in the picture. She could outwardly be the very funny person she'd been years before. Beside her husband, she was chastised into being quiet.

Maybe you've seen other women cautioned to keep themselves in minor roles to bolster their spouse's fragile ego. Maybe these women turned down career opportunities so they wouldn't exceed their husband's income, or perhaps they let friendships slide because he didn't approve. Personally, or even professionally, women sometimes put a lid on who they are in order to please their male partners.

If your partner chooses to be nasty, spiteful, and negative, that's his choice and his alone. You can rise above those patterns, however. You might want to call him a bottom feeder, but you can choose not to. It might irritate you that he can't even send the children home with a card for Mother's Day, but it doesn't mean you have to forget Father's Day.

Take the higher road. While difficult, you'll find it's usually the best course. Be who you are, and allow yourself to grow from the pain and hurt into your true potential, and someone you and your children can be so very proud of.

Helping Your Children

Speaking of the children, you might have thought we forgot about them in this discussion of separation and its immediate aftermath. But your children are very much in mind, for they are absorbing what goes on around them.

Don't feel guilty if you've focused on yourself for a while. Maybe upon reading this book, you've become more introspective. That's perfectly fine. Surviving separation reminds me of when the flight attendant cautions you to put the mask on yourself before trying to assist a young child. If you don't feel composed enough or capable enough to parent, a little time to regroup never hurts anyone. Soon your thoughts will turn to the little charges in your care, or the grown children equally troubled by the dissolution of their intact family.

Even when children enjoy time with both parents, they struggle. Anyone who doesn't recognize that it's harder for these children is living in deep denial. Imagine moving from place to place, remembering important belongings, missing the familiarity that comes with a home. It's something we adults take for granted once we establish ourselves in new housing, or stay in the dwelling we know as home.

Children aren't exempt from coming to their own conclusions. All kids want desperately to see their parents in a positive light. Coming to terms with someone's misdeeds is difficult for us adults. For the child who hasn't developed a full range of cognitive and emotional skills, it's nothing short of earth shattering.

When parents are openly hostile to one another, which is often the case before some cooling down occurs, the pain at seeing one parent treated poorly by another is immense. For that reason it's important to attempt civility, even goodwill toward an estranged partner. Try at least for the child's sake.

However, you can't make someone treat you well. Rest assured your children will learn important life lessons when goodwill is lacking. If dad fails to show up for his visitation time, he might intend to stick it to you, but he's really hurting his own reputation. Therapist friends I've talked with recall numerous clients who, twenty years later, remember when dad left them sitting with their coat and backpack.

My own preschooler, upon noticing it was a gift-giving occasion, commented, "I don't think dad likes you." My son knew I would always send them with a gift at Christmas, on their dad's birthday, or on Father's Day. I did this not to receive in return but because going empty-handed hurts a child, and it speaks volumes about values we're trying to impart. Incidents like this remind me to be who I want to be, and not to worry about the choices other parties make.

Probably the hardest task, ranking up there with your own evolution through this separation journey, is to see how your children struggle as well. This is a time to keep consistency, offer more hugs, and affirm that you will always love them and be there for them. In a child's mind, if one parent can walk out on the family, so can the other. Their security has been shattered. Never forget how important reassurance is to children of all ages.

What to Tell Children

It's everyone's favorite neighbor, Fred Rogers, who often emphasizes that grownups are the ones charged with caretaking, and our children shouldn't have to worry who will take care of them. In his book *Mister Rogers Talks With Parents,* he encourages us to explain divorce as a grown-up problem. In addition, Rogers advocates a discussion of which relationships will change in a child's life and which will not. That's because children often worry that they won't get to see or have contact with the other parent.

Chapter 3 explores many other coping strategies for helping children through the separation. At the outset, however, there needs to be honest communication, or at least honest in terms of what the child can accept and handle. If left to guess about their family troubles, kids may resort to fantasy answers that are indeed a lot more frightening than reality, and not at all reflective of what will happen to them.

Imparting news of a marital rift is probably a lot like discussing sexuality in stages. Give them enough to satisfy their curiosity, and add a little more when the time is right. When they worry about the future, reassure them: "We'll work it out." They don't need to know anything more than the immediate future for right now. Reaffirm that you will be there for them, and this will help them adjust to almost anything.

When purely adult issues such as adultery are involved, choose your words carefully. For instance, "Daddy likes his new girlfriend better than us" might be what you want to say, but a more tempered "Your dad and I have different ideas about being married" is more general, yet still truthful.

Rest assured the discussions will be ongoing with a multitude of topics. One therapist advised a mom facing constant harassment to simply state, "Your dad's just tough to deal with sometimes." That pretty much validated everyone's perception. Kids know more than we realize. To ignore harassment or abuse, especially if the kids are present when it occurs, is a mistake. You don't want to teach children that you are someone's doormat. But running the father into the ground in a tirade would surely be a mistake as well. So stick with tempered honesty as best you can, and it should serve you and your children well.

Slowly but Surely

All of this advice might be extremely difficult to follow, particularly when you are ruled more by the heart than by your head. But I can't emphasize enough that what you do and say—in the early stages of a separation and in the days ahead—can and will be used against you.

Resist the temptation to give in to your emotions. Anger makes us act impulsively. Use your support system to vent your anger and hurt, or read the next chapter to initiate strategies such as exercise to help you cope.

The golden rule here is to think first, mull it over some more, and then act accordingly. So you get legal letters in the mail, or you hear bits and pieces through the grapevine. This doesn't mean you should pick up the phone, dash off a nasty e-mail message, or incite legal action of your own. You might ultimately decide to respond, but if you think first, sleep on it (or at the very least give yourself a break from dealing with it), and then move forward, your actions will be less likely to haunt you, and more inclined to help you through this journey.

The Road Ahead

As you step out, prepare for the worst, and be surprised by the best. Sure, separating could be amicable. One husband insisted on paying spousal support so their children could continue to have a stay-at-home mom. But there aren't too many men like this (and it makes a case for cloning, doesn't it?). Ahead, you'll face unknown challenges. There will be tough times, and memorable ones. Indeed, if you're like me, there will be deciding moments that shed clear rays of light on old issues, helping you to decide your outcome.

Top Ten Practical Moves to Make When Separation Is Imminent

If you have an inkling that separation is headed your way, peruse this list. Call it looking out for number one, but if you don't—trust me—no one else will. Don't feel guilty about taking these measures if you must. And if you are dealing with domestic violence, turn to Chapter 5 for additional strategies.

1. **Knowledge is power.** Know where you and your husband have bank accounts, life insurance policies,

mutual funds, certificates of deposit, all other instruments of finance, and important documents such as social security cards, passports, birth and stock certificates, and the details of his pension, 401(k), and other employee benefits. Know the location of and have access to safe deposit boxes. Your county recorder of deeds can help you track down real estate and deeds.

If your marriage is just short of the ten-year mark, you may want to wait it out, if you can and if it's safe. You'll have more bargaining power in matters such as alimony, social security, pension benefits, and more. This is because courts tend to view marriages lasting at least ten years or more as longer term. Therefore, you may be eligible for a portion of your husband's pension and social security benefits (when you reach the age to claim these), and you may qualify for alimony. It's all good reason to speak with an attorney before moving out, or asking him to.

2. **Become a financial sleuth.** Obtain statements and balances for bank accounts, plus copies of wills and trusts. Make duplicate copies of computer files with financial data. The Social Security office can give you a current report of earning for both of you. Collect as many of your husband's pay stubs as possible. In some professions there are multiple paychecks. For instance, a police officer might receive separate payment for his court appearances. Or there could be bonuses or commissions accounted for on separate pay stubs. Most of this shows up on a W-2, but this doesn't help if it's July.

3. **Safeguard heirlooms and liquid assets.** Seek appraisals for artwork, antiques, and other collectibles. Take any sentimental or important objects to a friend's house for safekeeping. Be certain that your name is recorded on the house deed or apartment lease. Do not stash cash in a safe deposit box; for pending litigation, boxes are sometimes sealed. Make sure you revoke any powers of attorney your spouse may have and ask brokerage firms to check for identification before your name is signed to anything.
4. **Open a bank account in your name.** It only takes one party to raid an account, and you don't want to be left without any money. Certainly do not deposit any more of your own money into a joint account, even if you transfer that into your own name. Establish a new account for future deposits, preferably at another bank. This is where you can keep an emergency fund to live on and pay legal bills, at least until support is established. Don't be surprised if a spouse petitions for joint accounts to be frozen, pending equitable distribution in a divorce. This is another reason to have your own access to funds.
5. **Establish credit in your own name.** As soon as separation takes place, cancel or report missing jointly held credit cards. Then, go out and set up new accounts in your name only.
6. **Pay as many bills as possible.** Do this prior to separation so that you are not stuck with the obligations, risk having utilities shut off, or fight off a bad credit rap.

7. **Take care of household or car repairs.** If you've been putting these off, make that upgrade, such as air conditioning, a driveway, or a patio, particularly if you are fairly certain you will maintain and live in the residence at settlement. If you currently have an old vehicle and can afford to upgrade your set of wheels, do so. You'll need transportation, and as long as the expenditure is modest, you won't be faulted for a new (or slightly used) car. Indeed, if there is a manufacturer's warranty, you'll save money in years to come.
8. **Look after your health-care needs.** Visit your doctor for a routine checkup, annual OB/GYN exam, vision testing, or dental cleaning and x-rays. Chances are good your health-care coverage will remain in force for at least several months longer, but you might be responsible for any co-pays or procedures that aren't covered. So see to these visits now, and order any dental work or new glasses or contacts if they would be covered on your health plans.
9. **Invest in a better work wardrobe.** I'm not suggesting that you buy out Saks Fifth Avenue, only that you purchase some basics to see you through job interviews and career commitments. Focus on a few good suits and the appropriate accessories. But hey, a new bathing suit could do wonders for the self-esteem as well!
10. **Stock the pantry.** This might sound silly, but if funds get tight (and if you're dealing with a belligerent husband, they just might), you won't need to spend as much on groceries if you've stocked the pantry and filled the freezer.

Chapter Two

Looking after You

We were "learning to separate our lives." This was a line I kept hearing over and over when my marriage collapsed to the point of separation. I hated the thought. I grasped at any piece of my marriage that might have been worth saving. Unfortunately, I did this to the detriment of myself.

Over a span of four months, I lost fifteen pounds from stress. You have to realize I'm thin to begin with. I was too tense to eat well, and as a friend confided, "Loriann, you don't have fifteen pounds to lose." Sure, I fit into something slinky that Christmas without a problem, and I snarfed down those lasagna leftovers my friends had brought me, free of any guilt. But I'd rather not have gone through those emotional struggles.

Oddly enough, the line I abhorred quickly became my mantra in the weeks and months ahead. I was learning to separate my life from that of my husband. While I remained open to a possible reconciliation for several weeks, I wanted to be strong, at first for my children, but more important for my own self-worth. In a matter of months I realized there would be no reconciliation. This chapter will help you be strong for yourself regardless of your marriage's ultimate fate. Its focus is you—your well-being and your health.

Shattered Self-esteem

There are worse things than being separated. Truly, there are. As I looked at my life and career in those days, I saw a scared young woman with battle scars, hardly able to support herself, let alone two children with special physical, emotional, and learning needs. Friends kept telling me that I was strong, that I deserved better than what I was getting in my marriage, and that I had options.

For women who have endured years of verbal abuse, and for those who have been stunned with the shocking news of their husband's secret love affairs, or other illicit behavior, mending the self-esteem is a first step to solid ground. Some women have flat out been told they weren't attractive or desirable. They've listened to a long litany of deficits their partner perceived them to have. Other women are hurt to think that their husband wants to get rid of them so much that he'll be overly generous, as if they can't wait to have it over. Worse yet, many women who face marital separation say to themselves, "What did I do to cause this?" or "How stupid I was to waste the best years of my life!"

Wait a minute! No one—I repeat, *no one* is responsible for another person's behavior, choices, or decisions. We are responsible for our own lives. Too often as women, we feel the burden of making relationships work. When they fall apart, we're the first to accept the blame. This notion must end.

The message here is to stop clinging to your marriage and to goals, hopes, and dreams you set as a couple. Especially if one partner wants out of the marriage or refuses to correct patterns that have become major roadblocks, the sad truth is that there's nothing left upon which to build.

As Oprah Winfrey was addressing a graduating class, she said, "It doesn't matter what you've been through, where you come from, who your parents are or what your social or economic status is. None of that matters." She went on to add that it's how you choose to live, how you choose to love and give to others that really matters.

These remarks speak to me, with a message of hope and the permission to be a little selfish too. Who you used to be isn't necessarily who you will be in all your years to come. With emotional strength training, you can change. Your job is to take care of you, because if you fail to, I assure you that others won't do as good a job. And again, it's not their responsibility. It's yours.

If your husband and your marriage seemed to be the center of your life, these efforts of change and rebuilding will be more difficult. Even if you decide to reconcile with your husband, it's probably best to have your own life, your own interests, and your own focus. Men generally want to share their lives with women, not *be* their lives. Remember that, for whether you reconcile or find yourself dating in the years to come, you need to establish your own identity.

The Roller Coaster Ride

Where I live, we've got some classic roller coasters that could scare you good or send you on the best thrill of your life. That's the best analogy I can give you in the first weeks and months of separation. One day you'll be blue, feeling another frustrating false start. But the next day you'll wake refreshed, invigorated to tackle tasks, embrace life, and put your life back together. Here's how to have more of the latter and less of the former.

ALLOW YOURSELF TO BE ANGRY

So what that you're furious. As long as you don't hurt someone with that anger (namely, your children, yourself, or yes, even your estranged husband), give yourself the right to experience this emotion. You might have every right to be angry. Perhaps you've been lied to, cheated on, or battered about. I sought counsel from a trusted advisor when I felt I should be forgiving yet couldn't fathom how to do that. He said, "Maybe it's too soon to forgive." The first phase of separation isn't the time to compare yourself to Mother Theresa!

Now please understand. I'm not advocating that you allow your anger to run wild. You need to learn to channel your venom into positive energy that propels you forward and doesn't make you backslide. Journaling is one way of doing this. Venting to a friend or therapist is another. Two excellent resources for confronting your own anger are *The Dance of Anger* by Harriet G. Lerner, Ph.D., and *Healing An Angry Heart* by Cardwell C. Nuckols, Ph.D., and Bill Chickering.

Use your anger as a tool to get in touch with other emotions. In time, you'll discover the appropriate path for your angry feelings, which may turn to hurt, sadness, and even forgiveness. Ultimately, you will find that holding on to anger eats away at you, and that anger closes doors. Focusing on your own life in a loving way opens those doors to your future.

Let Go of Your Worries

These are probably plentiful right now. I truly know what it's like to be a dependent spouse, to be gripped by anxieties from household hassles to financial burdens. It's not the least bit fun when your mind is a jungle and your body too racked with worry to rest.

Yet there is an old adage that tells us that most of the things we worry about never come to pass. In many cases, our need to worry stems from our need to be in control. When you're suddenly separated, you don't feel in control at all. The key then is to focus on the issues we can directly influence, and then let go of all the rest.

Chronic worry saps energy, cripples creativity, and blinds us to real challenges. It can become disabling if we let it. "Worry is a core component of numerous medical disorders, and is central in many solvable, if not medically diagnosable, problems in life," says Edward M. Hallowell, M.D., a psychiatrist and author of the book *Worry: Controlling It and Using It Wisely.* Depending upon your circumstances, you might want to seek medical or psychological intervention to address your worries.

Go Ahead and Cry

This might not make sense on the heels of our trying to dump our worries. But indeed a good cry purges mounds of stress.

Some women have been taught to swallow their emotions and never let them show. Granted, if your crying scares your children or embarrasses you, then confine it to private moments. But let yourself go occasionally to have a good cry.

List What You're Thankful For

You've heard the popular expression "count your blessings." Well, by forcing yourself to list what you're thankful for, you do gain a positive perspective again. And what better time to do that than after you've had a good cry.

A close friend of mine had been divorced years before me so she understood exactly what I was going through. We'd often recite to each other the top three things we were thankful for whenever we got a little down. Even if the items on our list were as basic as having a roof over our head, a car that was paid off, or a favorite television program, we discovered many positives. If merely listing out loud isn't concrete enough, try writing a journal. Author Sarah Ban Breathnach's book *Simple Abundance Journal of Gratitude* might get you started.

Realize that Friendships Can Mean Friend Shifts

As you've already discovered, having a support system of trusted friends is vital. In some cases, a friend shift will mean that some people side with your estranged husband. In other cases, you'll be surrounded by the loving support you need, but even this can make you uncomfortable if you feel you're receiving more than you're giving.

True, solid friendships are two-way streets. Each party contributes to the trust and bond that endures. Each gives back what he or she receives. But let's face it. You're in crisis mode here, so all the rules get thrown out the window. Don't add this to your worries, because in time you'll be the stronger person in your friend's time of need.

People who have many good friends are physically healthier and live longer than loners. It's also well accepted that those with too few friends suffer from lower self-esteem. But what's a woman to do if friends aren't close by, or have drifted away? True friends are only a long-distance shoulder away, and with e-mail these days, it's so convenient to communicate to our heart's content. If you feel some friends have deserted you, it's time to form new friendships. Put yourself in the company of upbeat, warm-hearted people. Certainly, gathering places like church, school, work, neighborhoods, volunteer organizations, or even the parents of your children's social circle are all starting points to foster adult friendships.

Don't be surprised, though, if some friends can't handle your separation, for it reminds them that their own marriages could be headed for hard times. Rather than acknowledge their own fear, they deny your troubles, and your friendship is frayed. Limit your time around old friends who are not positive. If invited to get together with a less-than-cheerful person, merely decline. Right now you need understanding and peace of mind. You don't need hassles with difficult people when you already have enough of those with your husband.

Male Friends

When my marriage fell apart, I first turned to trusted girlfriends to dry my tears and lend an ear. But I soon realized how important it can be for women to have friendships with men.

Granted, a few of the guys I'm friendly with are husbands of my female friends. But not all. Men I've met through my career, church, or mutual friends remain confidantes and trusted allies.

Let's face it, raising two boys, dealing with an ex-husband, and dating again, I can turn to these buddies for a completely different perspective. Somehow, I think they reap a few benefits also. You'd think most women might be too—dare I say—chatty? Yes, we women do talk more. But when I held back on e-mail to one of my guy friends fearing just that, I got a long-distance call with the disappointed grumble, "But my screen is blank!"

Honestly, it's nice to be appreciated by members of the opposite sex, particularly when you've been disillusioned by your marriage partner. While a girlfriend can agree with my take on things, it's altogether a different validation when a guy says, "He was nuts for leaving you" or "You look great!" Some male friends have even confided that they've earnestly tried to rebuild my trust in men. I really appreciate that. It's sweet, if not a pure public service!

So learn to rely upon guy friends, not merely to help you set up the Christmas tree or fix a leaky faucet. Enjoy their support, their compliments, and for sure, learn all about the mysteries of testosterone.

Moral Matters

In a good many separations, one spouse or the other is tackling a moral dilemma. For instance, you discover your husband's addiction to alcohol or drugs, gambling, or even sex. On the other hand, you may have taken a male friendship too far into the realm of infidelity yourself.

Betrayal often forces problems in the marriage or with the individual out into the open. By betrayal, I don't mean sexual infidelity exclusively, but this is the most common culprit.

Who you were yesterday doesn't define who you will be tomorrow. If you feel ashamed by a personal failing, there's no need to add to your burden. The important thing is to take responsibility for what you've done and move on. If you've been the victim of betrayal, I understand that the hurt is very real. For most women, honesty is the bottom line. When that trust is broken, the damage seems irreparable.

So much discussion has surfaced ever since major Hollywood celebrities and political figures were caught in moral dilemmas. It's almost commonplace to hear of a husband's sexual compulsion. But just because it's in the headlines doesn't make it any less of an important issue to your marriage. You can't talk your way out of a situation you behaved your way into.

So how do you handle your man's affair or trysts on the seamier side of life? That's fodder for your therapist, for sure. But you do have options. Addictive behavior is usually only the first layer of a deeper problem. One should uncover the underlying cause. For some men who have one affair after another or pick up their women on the street, the real issue is not sex. And it's *not* your fault. The roots of compulsive sexual behavior can range from the need for power over another person, deep-seated anger, low self-esteem, and ego gratification to excessive risk taking, a genuine fear of emotional intimacy, low levels of dopamine in the brain, or even personality disorders.

This long list doesn't absolve anyone; we have choices over our behavior. Many people might suffer problems but choose more moral paths.

The person at fault should address the cause and make restitution if there is any hope for reconciliation. No remorse speaks volumes. Don't allow his behavior or guilt to damage your self-esteem.

Think about whether you are co-dependent. Really examine whether you are enabling poor behavior by denying it. Co-dependent partners often believe they are helping in some way when they truly perpetuate the destructive behavior. If you're overlooking and covering up for abuse, alcohol, drugs, gambling, or serial sex, you need to stop.

Hold your head high, deal with your partner's denial (or your own), and feel the hurt. You'll have plenty of questions. This is normal. You'll likely experience another stage where the anger takes over, followed by acceptance that this wasn't your fault. Only then can you begin to put closure to such a crisis. Couples can survive betrayal, and the episode might even strengthen their marriage.

Reawaken Your Spirit

Reliance upon a higher power and a personal relationship with God helps many women facing the crisis of separation. When it seems you can't make sense of your marriage, turning problems over to God might be reassuring. There were many Sundays I sat in church frustrated and feeling lost. I remember walking away in tears and apologizing for them to my minister. He replied that there was no better place to be than in the company of my church family. And he was right.

As difficult a journey as separation is, you might find it brings you closer to others, closer to yourself, and closer to God. There are some religions that frown upon the dissolution of a marriage, and some pastors who urge you to remain together regardless of the circumstances. I personally believe this must be an individual decision. Vows are important, but sometimes marriages must end. If your pastor is leading you in a direction that isn't wise given your circumstances, perhaps you need to find another church where you feel more understood.

Another problem occurs when one spouse wants to annul the marriage and the other is opposed to it. Sheila Rauch Kennedy chronicled her story in *Shattered Faith: A Woman's Struggle to Stop the Catholic Church From Annulling Her Marriage.* If your struggle is similar, perhaps this book will give you strength.

Of course, "How could God let this happen to me?" is a common question when you're feeling rather weak and neglected. You might even have trouble praying. Read with care the sections in this book about managing anger, in Chapters 2 and 9, for you might just be mad at the world, and in this case, mad at the God you worship. If you are a person of faith, admit your struggles with God to your friends, and if they are spiritually minded, they'll intercede for you in that department. Just know that plenty of other women before you have found hope in their faith, and you might too.

Books of prayers, daily devotional guides, and the Bible can offer you great strength and help you along the path of spiritual reawakening. Another book unique in its search for answers is *In The Meantime: Finding Yourself and the Love You Want.* Author Iyanla Vanzant uses the analogy of putting a house in order, showing what it takes to learn from the meantime experience—to get out, stay out, and move up to a better place.

Seeking Therapy

Our quest for greater understanding of what's happening to us can often move forward with the help of a trained professional. There are many types of counselors, and if you're a person of faith, you might choose to discuss matters with your minister or rabbi. But a psychologist or master's-level social worker, trained in counseling individuals, is perhaps your best bet.

You might already be familiar with counseling if you and your husband sought marital therapy prior to separating. As a general rule, therapists who worked with you as a couple will prefer that you seek another counselor for individual sessions. However, if enough time has lapsed between the marriage therapy and your own needs at present, then it's largely up to you and the therapist involved. If there are issues involving domestic violence or any form of abuse, women need to seek individual counseling to see things more clearly and remain safe in expressing themselves (see Chapter 5 for further insight).

You can find licensed psychotherapists through hospital referral lines, trusted friends, clergy, or your health plan. Many therapists make coming to sessions very convenient, offering evening and Saturday hours. If cost is a concern, inquire with your health plan to make sure you are using a provider within the network, or if necessary, ask counselors if they use a sliding scale.

It's very wise to begin therapy in the initial stages of a marital separation. I can't stress this enough. Most likely, you are still covered under your husband's health plan (unless you carry your own coverage). Once you divorce, cost may be a factor, and mental health coverage is frequently not rendered with less expensive policies.

Different types of psychotherapy suit different people. There's cognitive therapy, a behavioral approach, or a combination of techniques. In addition, group therapy might be effective in treating substance abuse or other addictions and in recovering from domestic violence.

Remember that many people call themselves counselors. When choosing a counselor ask about credentials and education. Is the therapist a licensed social worker or licensed psychologist? A doctorate degree in psychology isn't always necessary, but it is indeed an indication of advanced study. How long has the person practiced? Does he or she specialize in working with a particular type of patient? If you get the feeling that this counselor, after a few sessions, is promoting a separate agenda, beware. This can be the case with some religious-based counseling. Ideally, you want someone who has had patients going through marital separation or divorce. If you have other concerns, such as domestic violence, eating disorders, or depression, it's best to find a professional who is experienced enough to help you.

Women often feel more comfortable discussing personal details with a female, but the gender of the counselor is less important than your comfort level. If you begin therapy with a professional and don't feel at ease with that person, then find someone with whom you click. The length of treatment will vary according to your needs. Some patients find remaining in therapy quite productive because it gives them a sounding board and trusted advisor they may not otherwise have. Of course, if you ever feel pressured to follow advice that you aren't comfortable with, this is another sign you may need to change therapists. A good counselor doesn't actually tell you what to do as much as guides your thoughts to discover the right path yourself.

It's not uncommon that you might be plagued by anxiety or even depression. Individual counseling is often your first course of treatment, but if the symptoms are severe enough, you should seek a medical opinion. If you have suffered a fluctuation in weight, have persistent feelings of emptiness, experience difficulty maintaining your daily routine or sleeping through the night, or feel you might harm yourself or someone else, seek medical care immediately.

Your psychologist can recommend a psychiatrist, a medical doctor who can prescribe appropriate medications to alleviate your symptoms. Of course, you can always discuss what's going on in your life with your primary care physician. While you may feel like the only woman in the world bringing concerns of a troubled marriage to the exam room, I can assure you that doctors are accustomed to helping patients through these rough spots. Thus the referral system works both ways. Your primary care doctor can recommend a good therapist, and if you already have one, that counselor can help you find the appropriate medical practitioner to prescribe and monitor medications while you continue therapy.

Don't feel stigmatized if you do require anti-anxiety medication, anti-depressants, or a temporary sleep aid. You're going through a tough time, and if you can get a better night's rest to tackle the next day with more focus, then this is a good thing. Chances are, it's only temporary.

Establishing a Proper Diet and Exercise Regimen

At a time when you are filled with shock and stress or even newfound freedom and gladness, nourishing your body may take a back seat. But it's important to maintain a good diet with the nutrition that will energize your body and mind rather than make you sluggish.

Too Busy to Eat Right

You may shirk the responsibility in part because you lack the time to read labels or prepare proper meals. Grabbing a hamburger at the drive-through window, or heating up a frozen entrée might be the easy route to lunch or dinner. Skipping breakfast might even become the norm, especially if you haven't slept well the night before and are running late. However, you owe it to yourself to practice good eating habits. I guarantee it won't consume much time, but it will yield more energy and an overall feeling of wellness for you.

When I'm in a hurry, I am tempted to purchase more processed foods, grab easy-to-heat snacks or entrées, microwave a packaged bag of popcorn (versus air popping), and open cans of soup. Unfortunately, these types of foods are loaded with saturated fats, hydrogenated shortenings, sodium, and empty calories. By scheduling my time productively, I can add better selections to my grocery cart and combine food preparation with another activity, such as watching the evening news or enjoying a music video. Often it only takes setting aside a block of time to cut up veggies, make no-fat dip, or throw soup ingredients in the slow cooker, and the effort yields leftovers for the week.

The latest food pyramid illustrates that we should be introducing six to eleven daily servings of bread, natural-grain cereals, rice, or pasta into our diets along with three to five servings of vegetables and two to four different fruits. Toward the top of the pyramid, you'll find two to three servings of red meat, but also fish and poultry (white meat is best), dry beans, eggs, and nuts. You also need dairy requirements of two to three servings of skim milk, nonfat yogurt, and low-fat/low-cholesterol cheese and other dairy products. Fats, oils, and sweets should be used sparingly.

Those fats and oils not only contribute to a thicker waistline but raise your LDL levels (the bad cholesterol) and put you at greater risk of heart disease. Too little fiber and roughage in your diet leads to colon and other cancers as well as heart disease. Fine, you might say. But let me get through this crisis and then I'll worry about good nutrition. I say begin now. Reap the results of good nutrition today and tomorrow as well as in the years ahead.

CURB THE COFFEE HABIT

Here's another vice in times of added stress—caffeine. Oh I know, it's a tough one to cut back on. But caffeine adds no nutrients (the little bit of milk or cream does not count!), and it does dehydrate you more quickly. Instead of coffee, tea, or colas, make a pitcher of lemonade from frozen concentrate. At least the pulp adds a little fiber to your diet. If you must have a hot drink, warm milk with just a touch of coffee or brew a pot of decaf coffee or herbal tea. Or make coffee weaker by purchasing the caffeine-reduced blends. These are all much better beverage choices.

Of course, nothing replaces the value of plain old water, flavored with lemon slices if you want to fancy it up. Water is greatly underestimated and unappreciated according to *Dr. Nancy Snyderman's Guide to Good Health*. Snyderman, the medical correspondent for *Good Morning America*, explains how important good hydration is especially as we grow older. Water helps lubricate body linings, which change with hormonal fluctuations, and it does the same for joints. This literally makes you feel better. Water brings oxygen, nutrients, and hormones to our cells and carries away waste products via the bloodstream and lymphatic system. In addition, remaining well-hydrated means having better digestion and less dry skin. So you can see that even though good nutrition plays an integral role in our lives as we age, it has benefits today. What better time to start feeling better than now, when the rest of life seems out of order.

Necessary Supplements

Even if you eat a balanced diet of at least three good meals and healthy snacks in between, you'll likely benefit from a good multivitamin. Women often require higher levels of certain vitamins and minerals than men, especially iron and calcium. During times of high stress, keeping your resistance up is critical. Therefore, choose a brand of multivitamin that's suited to meet your needs as a woman. In addition to the calcium and iron, you might also want the B vitamins (said to help alleviate premenstrual symptoms), as well as vitamins A, C, and E, which are antioxidants and reduce the risk of heart disease and, perhaps, stroke.

An excellent resource for understanding nutrition as well as women's medical issues in general is the *American Medical Association's Complete Guide to Women's Health*. In addition, while the release of *Our Bodies, Ourselves* may have seemed radical thirty years ago, it's a well-respected tome for increasing awareness about women's health, sexuality, aging, and other issues.

Get Moving

People exercise for a variety of reasons. Chief among them is the desire to lose weight, and simply feel better physically and emotionally. Through exercise, our brains release endorphins, feel-good chemicals that give us a sense of well-being. Hard to believe that working up a good sweat can help reduce depression, anxiety, and mental clutter, but it does.

Before you begin to perspire, however, I'd recommend that you learn as much as possible about fitness and strength training. Seek the approval of your doctor if you're undertaking a diet and fitness program that might tax your stamina or physical condition. After the go-ahead, read articles or books by credentialed professionals on health and fitness. One such book is *Strong Women Stay Slim* by Miriam E. Nelson, Ph.D., with Sarah Wernick, Ph.D. Their book offers health, fitness, and nutrition information complete with recipes. Also, sign up for an aerobics class through a community college or the YWCA. Some health clubs and gyms even sponsor free orientation sessions or one-time consultations.

Working out with a friend is a real catalyst for changing your sedentary ways. Just don't compare your progress with hers. And don't be ruled by the bathroom scale; muscle weighs more than fat, so you may not see results in the numbers. Take a tape measure to your waist or hips and use clothing as a gauge of progress.

To stave off excuses that make you miss your exercise routine, have a gym bag ready in your car or near the front door. I do understand that not everyone can afford membership at a fitness facility. In that case, use these strategies to get moving and feel better at the high school track, or around the neighborhood.

CHOOSE A FAVORITE SPORT

If you enjoy it, this increases the likelihood that you'll continue your fitness commitment. Always warm up a few minutes before earnest exercise to prevent injury. Again, community colleges and municipal recreation departments offer seasonal tennis or swimming, self-defense classes, or other sports involving lessons or league play.

WALK OFTEN FOR A BRISK THREE TO FIVE MINUTES

Intersperse a minute of super fast walking. Follow this with a brisk walk again for a few minutes, and then another minute of picking up the pace. These sixty-second spurts of energy help you burn more calories. In inclement weather walk around the local indoor mall. You'll find you aren't alone.

DON'T TAKE THE EASY WAY OUT

Force yourself to take the stairs. Walk a longer distance from your car to the store. Mind the leash when Rover needs a walk. Any activity that gets you out of the sitting or resting position counts.

WORK OUT BEFORE EATING

This not only reduces your appetite but increases the calories your body burns during digestion. Never exercise on a full stomach.

USE FITNESS VIDEOS

Borrow a fitness video from the library or buy your own copy. Just be sure that the tape you invest in has solid guidance from a fitness professional and isn't merely celebrity fluff.

DANCE THE NIGHT AWAY

Turn on your favorite tunes and let yourself go for a good twenty to thirty minutes of intense dancing. Who knows, it just might boost your confidence on the nightclub floor!

STEAL OPPORTUNITIES OUT OF YOUR DAY TO FLEX THOSE MUSCLES

This might mean walking on your treadmill while on the telephone, riding the exercise bike, or doing crunches while watching television. It could mean doing squats while brushing your teeth or waiting for the laundry to cycle. Whatever works for your schedule works for your body.

GET PROFESSIONAL GUIDANCE FOR STRENGTH TRAINING.

Then relax a day in between sessions to give your muscles a chance to rest. It's during this rest time that muscle building actually occurs.

Alternative Therapies

Plenty of people take a holistic view toward their health and wellness. Several of the suggestions listed here for taking care of yourself and decreasing stress may seem commonplace to some people, indulgences to others.

Talk about taking things for granted. When you're suddenly separated, you do discover the loss of certain things. One of these is the power of touch. I don't merely mean a sexual relationship, but more important, a hug, a hand held, or a snuggle under the covers. Massage therapy offers an outlet for those who have lost the sense of touch. Studies at the University of Miami Medical School's Touch Research Institute have shown that massage reduces anxiety and lowers the body's production of stress hormones. The health benefits are substantial to diverse groups, including premature infants, babies, and people with certain medical conditions. So don't feel embarrassed by your desire to head off to a spa. You're perfectly normal.

Ask for personal recommendations to find a licensed or certified practitioner. Look in the Yellow Pages under "licensed massage therapist," not "massage parlor." When you go for your appointment, state your preferences, including whether you prefer to remain partially clothed in a bathing suit. You should always be draped with a sheet so that only the specific area being worked on is exposed. Do speak up if the massage is too uncomfortable. Finally, check your insurance plan; if massage therapy is prescribed by a doctor, it might be covered as treatment.

Of course, a day at a full-fledged spa could encompass all sorts of pampering, including facials and body wraps. But few of us can afford these luxuries. Instead, escape into your own bathtub with bath salts or oils, and let your mind wander. Add some scented candles to the room for aromatherapy. This is relaxation at its best! And while you wouldn't think that a deck of cards could do the trick for you, there is an entire fifty-two-card series published by Chronicle Books that just might perk up your spirits in very alternative ways. Lynn Gordon has made thumbing through her sets of *52 Relaxing Rituals* or *52 Ways to Mend a Broken Heart* fun reading. With a little innovation, your list of looking after yourself just got longer!

Other Health Issues

Other factors that contribute to your lack of overall well-being are the presence of nicotine, imbibing too much alcohol, and the absence of a good night's sleep.

There's no question that smoking is bad for you; it leads to cancer, ages you prematurely, and decreases your endurance. Give up the habit and you'll not only improve your long-term health but increase your stamina. When you're dealing with a lot of issues, this is a big incentive.

When life gets stressful, you might be compelled to enjoy a nightcap or glass of wine. True, there are health benefits to drinking red wine, in moderation. But too much alcohol will impair your mental functioning, increase the risk of certain cancers, and make you more prone to osteoporosis. An alcoholic drink may put you to sleep easily in the short term, but later cause you to awaken.

That brings us to the subject of sleep. A good night's rest will make even the most trying day much more bearable. To prevent a lack of sleep, look to environmental factors such as a poor mattress, too much noise near your bedroom, or temperature conditions. Besides anxiety and depression, sleep apnea, breathing disorders (such as asthma), or chronic pain can also be addressed by your physician.

Of course, stay clear of spicy, heavy, or fatty foods as well as caffeine in the evening hours. Choose warm milk, which contains a natural sleep aid.

Exercising in the late afternoon often promotes better sleep, as does a warm bath, a body massage, reading, or meditation. Remember, it's not the quantity of hours necessarily but the quality of one's sleep that matters most. If you've tried these approaches and still toss and turn, it's time to consult your doctor.

Your Husband and Your Health

It's unfortunate that just when you come to the emotional recognition of a husband's drug habit or extramarital relations, you must endure the added worry that you may have contracted a sexually transmitted disease, or possibly the AIDS virus. But you have to explore this possibility. "The problem is, in this day and age, a little indiscretion can kill you," says Mary E. O'Brien, M.D., author of *In Sickness and in Health.*

While hard to hear, Dr. O'Brien's advice is factual. If a woman even suspects infidelity, she should insist on protected sex only. She should be tested and insist that her husband is tested for sexually transmitted diseases including HIV and hepatitis. "If he is unwilling to comply, it should be clear that (a) he doesn't care about her health and safety; (b) he's selfish and inconsiderate; (c) he's irresponsible and immature; and (d) he has no idea what true love and commitment are all about," O'Brien adds. "That being the case, any self-respecting woman should insist on separation. Marital infidelity is no longer simply a matter of hurt feelings. It can be deadly."

Most of our fear centers around the fatal AIDS virus, but this is only one concern. A researcher from Johns Hopkins University School of Medicine studied the effects of unfaithful partners and found that their wives were five to nine times more likely to get cervical cancer if their husbands had multiple partners and contracted human papillomavirus (H.P.V). Of course, the more partners a woman has, the same risk rises. Since there are no physical symptoms of the H.P.V. virus, men who carry it are often clueless. In addition, if your husband has had multiple partners and subsequently had unprotected sex with you, your chances of developing a nuisance infection (such as a yeast infection) may also rise.

Thus, if you or your partner has engaged in high-risk behavior (sharing drug needles or syringes and/or engaging in sexual activities with others), ask your physician for a complete round of tests. Don't rely upon your husband's word that he is fine. Go yourself. Go today. It may seem humiliating, but physicians are accustomed to handling situations like this. Your office visit and testing is carried out in confidence. Should you test positive, you'll be referred to counseling to help you deal with the results. And in some cases, you may want to follow up with another HIV test six months later just to be sure.

To obtain more information about HIV transmission, practicing safe sex, and being tested, call the National AIDS Information line at 1-800-342-AIDS or the Centers for Disease Control's National STD hotline at 1-800-227-8922.

Dealing with Your Husband

Who said you can't live with them and you can't live without them? Well, part of me might agree with that when life is placid. But during your separation, it usually isn't. Therefore, we need to address how to deal with the men in your life. And truth be told, you *can* live without them.

Attorneys caution that you cannot have it both ways, at least if you want to preserve your legal position. You can't call yourself separated yet continue to have a sexual relationship, even occasional sex, with your spouse. The reason is simple. One of you could claim the marriage is not broken. For instance, if you proceed with a divorce down the road, you'll have to agree upon a date of separation. You may call that date the day he moved out of the residence. But if you've had relations, he may surface this fact in court and that date might be pushed back. If there is a legal waiting period before a divorce can be granted, and you decide you want it over with soon, then you're stuck. Thus, one brief moment of passion can set your case back. When engaging the heart, just make sure your head has a say.

COMMUNICATING

Shortly after my separation began, good friends of mine moved to another state. The wife, known for her sharp wit, was well-balanced by her easygoing husband. I'll never forget her advice on how to communicate with my estranged husband. "Construct watertight arguments," she'd say. "Don't give him any room to wiggle." When her husband concurred, I realized this was one of those teachable moments.

My friend had learned to stand up to bullies and passive-aggressive types. While she knew how to throw out a sarcastic line or give someone a good tongue lashing, she also appreciated when to relegate such diatribe to friends, not foe. I soon learned to implement her strategies into written and spoken communication.

If you're tempted to put emotion into your remarks, letters, or e-mail, I have only one word for you: *don't*. You must recognize that anything you say can, and most likely will, be used against you. Very often, if your spouse is in denial of his own poor behavior or of your resolve to end the relationship, no amount of language will get the message across. Still, you must communicate, particularly if you have children.

So how does one construct a watertight argument? Stick to the facts. Give only details, and never assume knowledge or understanding. It might seem exhaustive to restate times, locations, or circumstances, but you must. You never want to give your estranged partner the chance to reply with "well, I didn't know" or "that's not what I thought." For example, say you are e-mailing specific times and locations to pick up the children, and in this case the father is retrieving the kids from your parents' house. You know he knows where your parents live. You know he knows their phone number. You know he knows that 7:00 means in the evening. Doesn't matter. Spell out the address, give an emergency phone number, and put in the "PM" This covers you, and it gives the opposing party little room to wiggle.

The next communication caveat is a little harder to accomplish. Ignore the person's tone and nasty remarks. Still stick with the facts. And absolutely, positively, no sarcasm. None.

Now, if you think I didn't have a virtual field day inventing sarcastic remarks during my separation, just ask my friends. They tolerated some classic lines, and added a few quips of their own. But I've gradually learned to bite my tongue. Friends might get an earful later, but that's what friends are for. If you add venom and sarcasm to your communication with the other side, that's what you'll get back, ten times over. The two of you will be caught in a never-ending cycle of barbs that leads you nowhere constructive. And as a therapist offered, "The more you talk about something, the more mental energy you give it, and ultimately, the more it's still controlling your life." If you don't want your estranged husband influencing you in any way, then don't be a party to the nasty banter. Period.

Remember, an estranged spouse is usually an angry spouse, not thinking clearly and at times vindictive. And yes, in a marital separation there are two estranged spouses. Him, and you.

You can control how you communicate, and you can indirectly influence his pattern and tone by not going down a nonproductive path. It's no guarantee. But it furthers constructive communication, avoids frustration, and assures that whatever you say or write cannot come back to haunt you.

UNDERSTANDING PASSIVE AGGRESSION

A few years ago, the term *passive-aggressive* did not exist in my vocabulary. Chalk it up to my friend's experiences, and a few of my own, but now I've come to appreciate how to deal with passive-aggressive individuals, personally and professionally.

Army psychiatrist Col. William Menninger first coined the term *passive-aggressive* (P/A for short) during World War II. Soldiers following orders and coping with the lack of personal choice resisted, withdrew, and wanted to flee their dictates. Menninger labeled this resistance, for a P/A person thinks of himself as weak to those he perceives as more powerful. Thus, a P/A person easily transforms another into dictator status. It's hidden hostility under the guise of innocence or passivity.

Think about it. One woman shared that her estranged husband was supposed to transfer a vehicle they jointly owned into his name alone. They'd agreed to this, but he never followed through. Months passed. When the time came to register the car and have a state inspection, the wife didn't want responsibility for this vehicle. Communication got her nowhere, so she took the matter to court. When the judge ordered him to sign the paperwork, he blamed his wife for raising his legal fees and causing him to miss work. He failed to recognize his passive aggression.

As you communicate, try to recognize any P/A tendencies in yourself and realize that others who act this way have rather warped agendas stemming from their desire to control, or from interpersonal struggles. You aren't going to change them, but you don't have to accept responsibility for their issues either. Making their decisions and mitigating any consequences only teaches them to play the dependent role in the future. Furthermore, it fosters co-dependency.

Constructing watertight arguments works in combating P/A behavior as well. Be clear about your expectations. Set artificial deadlines. Don't back down no matter how much the person protests. Finally, decrease their waffling by asking attitudinal questions (questions that begin with "why" or "how"). The last thing you will get from a P/A person is a straight answer or direct response. Try to get their promises in writing.

The Temptations of Other Men

Sure, you're thinking. After dealing with difficult men, I want you to think about other guys! Well, not really. But getting back to the old "can't live without them" mode, I think it's important to address the allure of getting involved with other men at this stage in your separation. Again, at the risk of being a real killjoy here, I offer one word: *don't*.

If you're reading this book and you have already exited your marriage for the arms of someone else, you may be tempted to skip this section. Perhaps the two of you will beat the odds and grow happily old together in bliss. But on the chance that you are rebounding, please read on.

Rebounding is best explained in *Dating for Dummies* by Dr. Joy Browne, where she explains that this is no slam-dunk. Browne advises that one should not date until at least a year after any divorce has been finalized. I know this might seem like a long time when perhaps you might crave validation, affection, mere companionship, or even sex. But getting over a man isn't the same as getting over a dog. Replace Fido. Hold off on Harry.

Think about how dating might adversely affect your present case or any attempts at reconciliation with your spouse. "I have no intentions of getting back together," you might say. Fine. But I'd still hold off for several months, if not a year or two into your separation. Depending upon your state's laws, dating or "shacking up" during separation can be construed as fault, strengthening the other side's case. In addition, some states consider total household income in awarding support while others only include the income of the actual man and woman involved.

Whether you choose to wait out the sufficient time that assures you are interested in other men for the right reasons is your choice. But proceed cautiously and realize the risk of additional heartbreak and complications you don't need.

So if you don't date now, how can you find companionship? Get together with girlfriends. I loved the line in Dr. Browne's book where she writes, "Hang out with friends, large groups, small countries." It's true. It's easier that way, and you can still meet your social needs. Besides, you want to be fair to anyone you date. Wait until you have something to give. This might mean being patient while you tend to yourself, your children, legal matters, getting your career or finances together. But it will be worth the wait.

Chapter Three

Coping with Your Children

After the reality of marital separation hits parents, it turns next to the children. Where there has been ongoing discord or public knowledge of a marital misdeed, the news won't be a complete shock to older children. Kids are savvy enough to sense trouble.

But even if your children are clued in to your struggles, they will be affected by the breakup of their family unit. Your emotions will surface as well. It's hard to restrain what you're feeling in front of the children. Issues involving them tend to be triggers for us mothers, especially if estranged husbands aren't really considering the children's interests, but merely their own.

In addition, we are sometimes lulled into a false sense of security regarding custody. Thus, a word of caution here. While you may opt for an informal custody agreement between you and the children's father, you'll be much better off with a formal custody court order. Otherwise, each party has equal access to the kids. If there are true problems with your custody exchanges and the threat of violating your agreement, your order is enforceable by the police.

If you have children, this chapter will also give you an understanding into your child's world. It will alert you to common struggles kids face at various ages, for no child is immune to an emotional onslaught. Even college-age kids, living away from home, experience the impact of a marital separation. Reading further, you'll learn important strategies, from helping your children cope to dealing with a difficult estranged spouse and mediating child custody issues.

What the Experts Say

Fifty percent of first marriages and 60 percent of remarriages end in divorce. With a million new divorces each year, that's a lot of children living in the wake of their parents' bitterness. One in three children endures a family divorce by age eighteen, and you know there are plenty more struggling with a marital separation, before other couples reconcile.

Judith Wallerstein is an author who has conducted long-term research on the effects of separation and divorce. In her book *Second Chances: Men, Women and Children a Decade After Divorce,* she and her co-author Sandra Blakeslee noted that fifteen years or more following a divorce, many children have significant emotional fallout from their parent's warfare. While one tends to think a separation alleviates the discord, it's only the beginning of a truce, possibly years down the road. Sometimes that truce never occurs.

"Some children are relieved that the arguments may end with the parents' separation, but most children do not react this way," says Timothy F. Murphy, Ph.D. Dr. Murphy and I have written *The Angry Child*. Dr Murphy has helped hundreds of families in the Pittsburgh area as a practicing psychologist and also chairs a committee on youth issues as a Pennsylvania state senator.

"Children may act more frustrated, impatient, or anger easily," Dr. Murphy says. "They may become depressed, withdrawn, or moody. To cope with the stresses, a child may even deny their parents are splitting up."

One barometer Dr. Murphy uses is gauging the child's behavior before the separation. Whatever psychological symptoms exist before parents separate are good predictors of symptoms these children will have later on. These are children struggling to discover where they fit in, especially if it appears dad has run off to a new life or mom suddenly has a steady boyfriend. In their minds, perhaps, wasn't their original family good enough?

But does this mean children are ruined because two parents have perhaps realized their mistakes and chosen to create new futures? No, it does not. Parents can make the transition from co-partners to co-parents. They probably can't escape the pain of divorce; nor can their children. However, they can be sensitive to children's feelings, putting the kids first and learning to forge ahead to a more peaceful future.

Breaking the News

In *Vicki Lansky's Divorce Book for Parents,* the author likens the mention of divorce to your children with shouting "Fire!" in a crowded movie theater. And she should know. Having worked with her ex-husband in a publishing venture, Lansky went through not only a personal but professional divorce.

She makes the point that, to children, parents are a packaged deal, with no knowledge that the two of you ever had lives before the marriage and will move on to the same in the months to come. Kids never expect to have two homes, two sets of clothing, toys, and toothbrushes, and two sets of traditions and rules.

So how do you lessen the blow? Can you soften the news so that it doesn't hurt? The answer is, you can't. However, you can choose your words carefully and be as honest as possible about the pain.

Whatever you do, don't make light of the situation in front of your children. To your adult friends or to yourself, fine. Use caution with honesty. I know the temptation to tell all. One of the hardest comments you might listen to could be "Maybe if you and daddy didn't argue, he'd still be here." In some cases where there is obvious violence in the home or open courting of another woman, the children will see this behavior for themselves. Your best counter may be to acknowledge the child's pain with a phrase like "I know we argued. I had a right to be angry, and I know that's hard for you to understand. We didn't want to live that way, so we're living apart."

On the other hand, you don't want to enable your estranged husband's poor behavior by covering it up or denying it. Kids are too savvy for that. Where there has been domestic violence, for example, you can honestly say, "Your dad has some real problems with his anger. That's why we need to live apart." Still, rein in the urge to blame. You can be honest without crossing that line.

The most important aspect of conveying this distressing news to your children is the reassurance that the separation or impending divorce is not their fault. The second caveat is to reassure them that their needs will always matter, that they will always be taken care of, and that they are loved by both of you.

It's probably best to speak to all the kids as a group, even if there is a great age differential. Do this at home, not out in public. Use plain language. Kids hardly understand the word *divorce,* let alone *custody, lawyer,* or *court order.* Also, watch how you address money matters. To most children, ten dollars may seem a fortune, so they really don't need to know numbers. The exception might be if they are of college age, where they see the expenditures and have a truer understanding of finances. If there are some changes in lifestyle, you'll have to discuss these circumstances. Children accustomed to using the health club need to know you won't be renewing the membership. Merely state that you've decided to save money for now.

Finally, it goes without saying that you should never lie, bribe, or promise things you can't deliver. In one case, children were promised a puppy, as if that would replace their mother! Realize that this is a new juncture for you and your children. Their trust in the institution of their family has been broken. Don't fragment that even further by telling them something that is blatantly false.

How Children Feel at Different Ages

Family breakdowns and impending divorces can have major impacts upon every area of children's development, affecting their social, emotional, and learning skills. Some parents manage to soften the pain and successfully bypass problems. But even when parents try their very best, these kids experience higher rates of depression, acting out sexually, drug abuse, behavior problems, school difficulties, and delinquency.

So the bottom line is that most kids face some level of psychological difficulty. Children whose separated parents still play out their conflicts are at higher risk. And it's a fact that custodial parents do have their challenges. From the child's perspective, you haven't left them. Your love and acceptance is stable, and therefore there isn't the concern that you'll walk out because of misbehavior or backtalk. Unfortunately, you may see your share of both

Here is a glimpse of your child's other reactions, dependent upon age.

TODDLERS AND PRESCHOOLERS

Toddlers who sense a change in the air might react with a sense of helplessness, while preschoolers feel a great deal of guilt. They may blame themselves for the breakup: "Daddy left because I didn't clean up my room." If a child in a tantrum previously fantasized about not having parents, she may now feel her temporary wish came true.That's a lot for a little heart to bear.

Furthermore, small children worry about who will take care of them. One of the resounding messages I've gained from watching *Mister Rogers' Neighborhood* with my sons is that no child should ever have to worry about this. Fred Rogers' song "I'm Taking Care of You" pretty much sums that up. In fact, Rogers' company, Family Communications, has compiled a booklet to help parents titled "Talking With Families About Divorce." (see appendix for more information.)

Very young children who seem to have conquered particular milestones such as potty-training may regress during family conflict and upheaval. These children may appear more whiny or cling to a parent just when you thought separation anxiety had been mastered.

Elementary and Middle School Children

School-age children often respond with significant anger or sadness, sometimes culminating in childhood depression. Let's face it. A preoccupied parent is one with a diminished capacity to parent effectively. A parent's own depression makes it difficult to console a child's anxiety. Some children then take on the role of their mom's or dad's caretaker—a clearly inappropriate response.

Crying and sobbing are not uncommon. Fears run wild. For instance, if your family experienced domestic violence, your children will worry about you, their mother, and your personal safety. For years, my oldest son worried about our house at night. He'd remind me repeatedly to set the alarm system, and he'd come into my room to check on me.

Children between the ages of six and twelve often react with greater rage as they witness the rancor between parents, especially as the separation moves to divorce litigation. Uncertain attempts at reconciliation in plain view of the children might give false hopes, for all children wish their parents would live happily ever after. If those hopes are dashed, it's a double whammy.

Similarly, some children try hard to get their families to reunite. Remember the movie *Parent Trap.* Children might be extremely helpful in hopes of rescuing their parents' marriage.

Since many children rely upon their family structure to help develop their identities, these youngsters are also frequently confused. They must deal with the threat of a ruptured identity when their parents separate.

Finally, don't be surprised if schoolwork is affected. Sometimes, children bury themselves in their studies just as adults do in their professions. If this occurs, grades may improve. All too often, however, grades suffer because kids can't concentrate or parents are too preoccupied to enforce good homework habits and school attendance.

ADOLESCENTS

Adolescents cope with their parents' separation by assuming an air of false maturity. Sometimes overwhelmed parents push these kids' needs aside, feeling that they can manage on their own for a while. But adolescents need love and affection even more because of their changing bodies and confusing thoughts. Thus, to seek approval or affection, it's not uncommon for a young girl to fall for the flirtations of an older boy, giving way to early sexual experiences she's ill-equipped to handle. It also explains why adolescents fall into the wrong peer groups or experiment with mind-altering drugs or alcohol.

Kids this age also cope with mixed emotions as they see their parents as sexual persons. It's a startling discovery for adolescents to watch their mom and dad show concern about appearance, begin to date, and become physically amorous with other partners. It can evoke vivid sexual fantasies in some children, embarrassment in others, and even cause a few to skip visitation with the sexually active parent. This doesn't mean separated parents aren't entitled to their own lives, but it does indicate the need for sensitivity and discretion.

Preteens might also feel hurried and pressed to quickly assume the independence that their peers typically achieve several years later. This frustrates them, for if they must look after a younger brother while you're at work or fix a sister's bike because dad isn't there to do it, they lack the leisure and downtime their friends have. Kids might view every extra chore or favor as a consequence of your separation and divorce.

Young Adults

As children mature and rational thinking increases, the group best able to cope is those age seventeen and beyond. This group is on the way out of the family unit, so to speak. They no longer require the protective structure of the family and can better empathize with their parent's individual needs.

However, this doesn't mean that separation and divorce aren't difficult on this group of almost-adult children. Especially if there are concerns about how to afford higher education, and again if there is open animosity between the parents, children at any age will take the family breakdown to heart. Their dreams of having happy parents at their wedding or even of having a set of grandparents for their own offspring are now dashed.

If there is any light to be seen regarding a parent's problem behavior, this age is when children will most likely recognize it on their own. For instance, the father who is quite capable of helping with college tuition yet withholds funds to irritate the mother can no longer rationalize his poor behavior to the kids. It just won't work.

Meeting Children's Needs

Separated parents who are preoccupied with their own emotional struggles, legal battles, and household tasks most likely see an abrupt departure from their own daily routines. Young children, in particular, need the structure of normalcy. Keep the kids' patterns as close to what they are used to as you possibly can.

As hard as it may be to juggle all the demands upon your time, try to carve out moments for individual attention and family activity. From the children's perspective, it seems that the family has fallen apart. So if your household now consists of yourself and your two daughters, show them concretely that the three of you still operate as a unit.

Of course, individual attention is crucial. Nothing replaces one-on-one time with a parent, but this is a challenge when you're playing mom *and* dad. Therefore, look to friends, relatives, and others to help out. Big Brothers/Big Sisters of America has local chapters to pair your child with a mentor. Visit the web at www.bbbsa.org or contact their national office in Philadelphia.

Your child's school or church might also help. One school counselor I know matches high school and elementary boys in a mentoring-type relationship where they assist with homework or simply play chess.

When I first was separated, a friend said, "Just give those kids a lot of extra hugs." I did. They needed them. As I stated earlier, touch plays an important role in feeling better. While a massage and spa day is more appropriate for you, your child will benefit by sitting close by, curling up to watch television or read a book, and, of course, by being embraced. Hugs do heal!

If you've tried all of this and continue to sense that your child is troubled, it's probably wise to seek professional help. Your son or daughter could very well be suffering from an anxiety disorder or depression, which if left unattended may get worse. Ask your pediatrician or school counselor for the names of qualified therapists or child psychologists. Call and interview these professionals. Sometimes having another caring adult listen to their struggles is all a child needs to bounce back. In other cases, your pediatrician may prescribe medication.

Setting Anger Rules

In collaborating with Dr. Timothy F. Murphy in writing *The Angry Child,* I've learned an important rule: It's sometimes okay to be angry, but never okay to be mean. Dr. Murphy points out that anger never exists on its own. There is always a trigger, and your separation is probably behind your children's negative feelings. Your goal isn't necessarily to repress or ignore your children's anger but to help them channel and direct it to constructive ends.

Anger may be a defense to avoid painful feelings, a sense of failure, low self-esteem, or isolation.These are additional triggers. Since a separation is a situation over which children have no control, their anger may surface out of the frustration. Knowing that, use the following guidelines in dealing with an angry child:

- Distinguish between anger that is a temporary state and aggression that is more profoundly an attempt to hurt a person or destroy property. Identifying the triggers helps here.
- Teach acceptable ways of coping with anger, for it's not enough to merely find outbursts unacceptable. Model these by reining in your own anger. Contrary to popular belief, punishment is not a very effective way to communicate your expectations.
- Reiterate to your children the messages that when angry, they cannot hurt themselves, they cannot hurt anyone or anything, and that anger has the potential for getting them in trouble. Ask them how they can express their anger in better ways. Encourage them to write and talk matters out. Venting with harsh words or thrown objects only teaches aggression.
- Steel yourself to hear such phrases as "I want daddy" or "I'll go live with my father." Kids know what buttons to press when you, and they, are angry. If you hear those words, ignore them. Most likely, they were spoken out of frustration.
- Catch each child doing something positive and tell them how proud you are. Kids facing the loss of a parent, an interrupted routine, and additional worries need to be reminded about what's good in their lives.

- Provide opportunities for children to exercise. Having a physical outlet like shooting hoops, riding bikes, or even taking walks curbs anger. Besides, it's healthy.
- Practice affection. Take time for calm conversation. An "I love you" before they leave for school starts the day off right.
- Diffuse tension through humor. A child who just yelled out in anger might be brought around as you lock eyes and break into a grin. This offers the child the opportunity to save face. Just be certain the humor is understood as such and not perceived as sarcasm or mockery.
- Help foster a positive self-image. Kids who feel valued and know of their contributions to their family and friends as well as their potential in school and outside activities can better handle anger. They are less likely to feel overwhelmed.

Handling the Tug of War

One mother facing the hassles of separation summed it up by saying, "If you think marriage takes effort, wait until you try divorce." Separating households and building new lives requires far more adjustment than most families face. When one parent or, heaven forbid, both parents refuse to work on adjustments, everyone is headed for trouble.

"Frequently, the adults are blind to their own anger," says Dr. Murphy. "They use subtle methods of undermining the child's relationship with the other parent." For instance, adults may refer to the other parent by first name rather than the title of "daddy" or "mommy." When their child complains about something, even minor, at the other parent's home, they immediately side with the child rather than support the other parent's authority.

Shelve your negative feelings toward your former partner as much as possible around your children. Admittedly, that's difficult. One of the hardest things mothers face is allowing children to have positive thoughts about a person they've seen at his worst.

It's best for everyone's sake if you find ways of communicating with your estranged spouse—whatever works for you, including e-mail, notes, intermediaries, or telephone calls. Don't place a child in the messenger role, and avoid grilling children for a play-by-play of their time with dad.

When parents wage war through their children, it sends a not-so-subtle message of "I am not able to handle this like an adult so I will have you [the child] do it for me." That places an adult burden on a child's shoulders. The kids already have added burdens with their family unraveling. Don't force them to carry more than they can bear.

Mediating Custody and Visitation Disputes

Formal mediation of child custody and visitation is popular, and in some jurisdictions mandatory. First, let's discuss exactly what mediation involves.

A trained mediator has a background in psychology, social work, or family law. This person doesn't take sides. He or she is there to help a couple define disputes, often because they are so blinded by bitterness or overwhelming emotion that they cannot think clearly. The mediator will help the two arrive at conclusions that they take to individual attorneys to become a court order.

Mediation is not a binding decision. But it does take place in an emotionally safe place, for most quarreling spouses calm down a little in the presence of a third party, at a neutral location. Sometimes, mediation involves attending educational seminars. Each parent pays toward the cost of these sessions.

There are good reasons to use a qualified mediator. For starters, the process emanates from a position of cooperation not antagonism. If you've already received nasty grams from your estranged husband or his attorney, you know exactly what I mean. Where does this get the two of you, and your children? Nowhere! Therefore, the mere act of going to mediation speaks volumes. As Vicki Lansky puts it, the lawyers then act more as advisors than gladiators.

Mediation also allows parents to make their own decisions regarding their own children. Everyone wants to believe that the courts will act in the best interest of the kids, and they do try. But let's be honest. No one has the breadth of understanding and background on these children that you and their father do.

Furthermore, mediation is less costly than dueling it out through attorneys and the courts. Slashing legal costs is discussed in Chapter 4, but mediation is long held by experts as a way to trim legal expenses.

However, while these are all good reasons to move forward with mediation, there are reasons to opt out of it. Where there has been an imbalance of power, such as with physical or verbal abuse, child abuse, or perhaps an addiction that impairs judgment, mediation may be useless. In fact, in my own hometown of Pittsburgh, victims of domestic violence can choose a waiver so that they need not encounter their abuser.

Hints for the Holidays

When my husband began living apart, it was late October. Stores already had holiday merchandise on the shelves. In a few weeks, I knew it would be that magical time I'd always looked forward to as my favorite season.

That year in particular, I made a promise to myself, but also to my children. I refused to allow the absence of my husband and their father to affect my enthusiasm for the holidays. I'm not saying it was easy, for I'm a fairly sentimental person. But knowing in advance that the season would have its emotional challenges, I was determined to decorate as usual, make our favorite cookie recipes, and get together with cherished friends.

No holiday is ever perfect, whether we're happily married or partnerless. The myth that everyone is supposed to be happy is just that—a myth. So set realistic expectations. Something invariably won't go as planned; if there is harbored anger over the separation, this is almost a guarantee. One woman found that her in-laws used that first holiday season to prove points. While they'd normally heeded their daughter-in-law's views on what was appropriate or inappropriate, they used the opportunity to purchase gifts they knew she was on record as opposing. Passive-aggressive acts like these do no one favors—certainly not the children caught in the middle.

As you can see, family issues get stirred up, and there's the potential for a lot of negative emotions. Do your best to keep the holidays pleasant, perhaps low-key so as to soften the fall to reality. Also, realize that your holiday—whichever your family puts the emphasis on—isn't merely one day. There's a whole season out there. Celebrate it to the fullest, in daily components if you must.

Separation Dos and Don'ts

When you have a baby, everyone is full of advice. The same goes as you separate. Here are some strategies to consider as you navigate the weeks and months ahead:

- **Do** reassure your children that your breakup had nothing to do with them.
- **Do** reaffirm that both parents love them and care for them. Even when you feel the other parent needs a dose of maturity, children need to know they are loved.
- **Do** maintain consistency and discipline. Too often parents relax the rules during a separation because they want to influence the child's loyalty or they're too exhausted to be firm. Consistency and discipline ensure stability.
- **Do** allow your children the right to their own emotions. Help them cope with all feelings, even the difficult ones.
- **Don't** flaunt new relationships and potential stepchildren in front of them. Some parents do this to replace the family concept they wanted to work so badly but

failed at. Others hope word will leak to their estranged spouse. It's not appropriate unless a long-term relationship develops. You shouldn't be dating in place of spending time with your kids. Besides, should your new beau depart, it's an emotional rerun for them.

- **Do** gain independence. Children benefit from seeing that both parents can cook, balance a checkbook, and mow the lawn.
- **Do** ask children to do age-appropriate tasks to help around the house. Preschoolers can keep their rooms neat, wipe their feet, put dirty clothing in the hamper, and set the table. As they grow, ask your kids to make their beds, clear the table, wash and dry dishes, rake leaves, and unpack groceries. Teens can prepare simple meals, wash clothes, and clean parts of the house (yes, even the bathroom!).
- **Don't** threaten to send kids off to their dad. In the event that you slip up, apologize quickly and reassure that you said things you regret.
- **Do** remember to be the parent. If you need a shoulder to lean on, try that of a friend, another adult, a minister or a therapist. Protect their childhood.
- **Don't** overcompensate by buying things and indulging your kids.
- **Do** realize that though you might dub your former partner a failed husband, he could be a successful father.

Tips for Noncustodial Parents

"Regular visitation is proof to the child that even though the marriage did not last, the love of the parent goes on forever," says Dr. Murphy. "When a parent drops out of a child's life and is inconsistent with visitation, or if a parent undermines the schedule of visits with the other parent, it's the child who suffers."

If you're the parent with visitation rights, understand the impact your actions (or sometimes lack thereof) have on your children. To a child, a promise is a promise. Children wait anxiously for the noncustodial parent to arrive. Understandably, work may prevent you from being on time, traffic may snarl your best efforts, and you do deserve to have a life outside of the parent-child relationship. But your commitment to your children is paramount. And it starts with the responsibility of spending time with your child as well as maintaining financial commitments.

Unfortunately, this is an area marred by late-show or no-show parents, often in an effort to infuriate their estranged partner or prove a point. Trust me—there is nothing worse than the sight of children, ready in coats and backpacks, eagerly looking out the window for a parent to pick them up.

I've heard of incidents where children were left at a restaurant because a parent got frustrated with them or kids having to sleep at dad's girlfriend's because it was more fun for him. And in yet another incident, one parent purposely showed up late or arrived early to tick off the former spouse or failed to communicate business travel plans.

Bottom line: Do what's best for your children. Especially if you are the noncustodial parent with precious little time to spend with them, put their needs first. Realize also that any rudeness you model leads to rude behavior in your child, and encourages acting out and backtalking as well.

Of course, the other matter involving noncustodial parents is child support. Women are just as likely in this era to earn greater incomes and pay support to estranged husbands who maintain custody. Child support is most always carried through with wage attachment, but if yours is not (because of self-employment or some other circumstance), make the payments on time. Also recognize that children deserve a few extras in this world. That means picking up the tab for the occasional haircut, summer camp, or swimming lessons. And certainly, don't grill your children on how their child support is spent.

Finally, it can't be easy to be separated from your children. There are ways that you can keep in touch, however. E-mail or telephone your kids on a frequent basis. Letters and notes are wonderful not merely on birthdays or Valentine's Day but throughout the year. This is especially important for children who are away at school without either parent to lean on. Care packages sent to dorm rooms are instant hits and speak volumes to their recipients!

Keep a calendar listing important dates such as open houses, parent days, and school vacations. If in doubt, contact your child's school counselor or principal (or in the case of older children, the university student affairs office) for such a list. Show up when you can. Your presence will be remembered for years to come.

Dealing with a Difficult Dad

I remember someone commenting about the books on my bookshelf, all lined up together. Titles like *The Wounded Male; Angry Men, Passive Men;* and *Dealing With Difficult Men* stood out to this person, who commented, "My, what a sign of the men in your life." Suffice to say, throughout separation and divorce, I think my bookshelf only expanded its collection.

Indeed, it's difficult to be an effective, happy parent if you continually feel you're hitting road blocks. It doesn't give you a secure feeling to know your estranged might have had six different addresses in half as many years. It's hard when you see them flaunt expensive lifestyles. It's devastating to watch a father drop out of a child's life when you know how much your son or daughter loves dad. It's galling when you discover that your children spent the night as daddy shacked up with his girlfriend. And it's scary when you realize your children's health or safety has been compromised by irresponsible judgment.

This kind of worry saps your energy—energy you'd rather put toward your children instead of legal battles or back-and-forth squabbles. But indeed, if there is real danger or concern, you must fight for your children's welfare.

When you have an adversarial relationship with your children's father, you're at a distinct disadvantage, for there is no one else to bounce ideas off of. If you don't trust the other parent to discuss strategies, at least consult another mom or dad you know—a person you trust who knows some background of your child and your situation.

Especially when you are trying to raise children with someone you know has some real issues to deal with, the struggle is even harder. As one mom at a women's shelter told me, "The same system that's supposed to help me get away from him keeps me intertwined with him."

If after all your best efforts to co-parent with a jerk there is still no cooperation, steal yourself to focus on your mission as parent. "Bring up your child with sound moral and social standards," says Dr. Murphy. "Try to give your children as strong a foundation as you can. If there is light to be seen, your children will see it someday."

Choosing Child Care

You'll likely need a reprieve for work or a sanity break with adult friends. I couldn't conclude without a discussion of finding appropriate child care.

The mere mention may be anathema to you, particularly if you had been a stay-at-home mom. You might feel guilty for considering the subject, but don't let your fears consume you. Lots of children thrive in child care. Perhaps you can't control the fact that you're separated, but you can select a quality arrangement that works for you and your child. Besides, your child may benefit from the active attention of another adult at this time when you're a little overwhelmed.

There are three main types of child care for working moms First, there's a private sitter in the home, usually a trusted friend or relative who can watch your child in your own house or in theirs. This could be a college-age au pair who comes to the United States. as part of an exchange program. A popular second is a licensed center. Another solution is the family day-care home where a child-care worker cares for several children in a private home.

In his book *Mister Rogers Talks With Parents,* Fred Rogers offers guidelines for selecting child care. For very small children, consistency of care matters most, as does the caregiver's experience looking after infants and toddlers. Look around to see that there are plenty of safe space to explore, a healthy atmosphere of books and toys, and opportunities for preschoolers to learn.

Most experts agree that the proper ratio should be no more than four infants to one adult, five toddlers to one adult, and ten preschoolers to one adult.

Ask about the level of education that providers have. What are the rates? Do they change as children get older? Are lunches or snacks provided? What activities are there for the children? What discipline methods are used? And, what's the turnover rate for the center's staff?

State and local governments license child-care centers. The National Association for the Education of Young Children (NAEYC) has an accreditation program for centers that exceeds the requirements of the best state regulatory systems. Such accreditation is not mandatory but a sign that the center is working hard to provide the best service. To find an accredited center in your area, call NAEYC at 800-424-2460.

For a family day-care provider, ask about registration with the state or local government and get a feel for this person's experiences with children. Is any extra help provided, and if so, who provides it? How many children are cared for total? How many days was the provider ill within the past year? Does he or she smoke? Are there any pets around? Are there any disabilities that would interfere with your child's care? How does the provider's family feel about children, and why did the provider offer child care in the first place?

Consider the physical surroundings, where the children eat, nap, play, and learn. Look for health precautions (frequent hand washing especially), child proofing, emergency procedures posted, books and educational equipment. Find out what activities go on and if the provider takes the children places (such as the library or the park). Finally, ask the caregiver how he or she would react in certain situations (e.g., if your child is choking, or when disciplining).

For those occasions when your child announces "Mommy, I feel sick," you may need to have a backup plan, especially if you fear that taking time off would jeopardize your job. In Pittsburgh, moms can preregister children with The Get Well Room at Magee-Women's Hospital, a separate area of The Children's Center of Pittsburgh. It provides a warm, loving place for a child to recuperate from mild illnesses such as sore throats, mild bronchitis, diarrhea, pain, and fever from vaccinations. If the center is not filled on the morning you call, your child can spend the day. Aides help the pediatric staff nurse, and activities are low-key, involving reading, watching videotapes, or sleeping.

Do keep careful records of your child-care expenses, for you might need proof of what your expenses are. Most jurisdictions require that both parents contribute to child-care costs.

Finding Baby-sitters

You will need to rely upon baby-sitters from time to time whether you use your own older children, a teenager, or an adult. Parents need to consider a sitter's age and energy level, the qualifications that go into baby-sitting, and any references provided. Simply put, are rambunctious toddlers going to wear out an older person or put teenagers to tests they aren't ready for? Whoever you choose should be able to handle a variety of situations, including feeding, bathing, and disciplining your children, as well as any emergency measures, such as choking rescue procedures, mouth-to-mouth breathing, and cardiopulmonary resuscitation (CPR).

As children get older, you can use teenage sitters; with very young children, you might feel more comfortable with adults. For overnights, you might prefer relatives. And if you have an older child capable of watching a younger sibling, enroll him or her in a baby-sitting class available at local hospitals or community colleges. This ensures that they'll know emergency procedures, and it instills confidence.

Perhaps you can find the help you need from mother's-day-out programs or personal referrals. Ask friends, day-care workers, or those in your church for recommendations. You could call upon youth groups, Girl Scout troops, or the YWCA to see if they have a list of qualified sitters.

Finally, a word to the wise. In one case of separated parents, when the mom broached the subject of child care and related expenses in their financial dealings, the dad countered with "I should be the one to watch the kids if you need a sitter." This is not always the best option.

For starters, your children might need to be settled in their own home, and that's a place you certainly don't want your estranged husband for many reasons. (See Chapter 5 if you have any doubts.) Furthermore, your estranged may leave you in a bind. It happens, particularly when you have a spouse vindictive enough to play games, jeopardize your employment, or foil your social life. My advice is to build a child-care network that includes trusted caregivers so that you don't need to rely upon the children's father.

Support for Single Parents

I know that raising your children alone is not what you had anticipated. When my separation began, my oldest son was struggling in first grade and my youngest was diagnosed with asthma in addition to the developmental delays most preemies encounter. I had my hands full. It couldn't have occurred at a worse time.

Now, years after that initial separation, there are moments I'm saddened that my children don't have the traditional family. Like you, this isn't what I wanted for them, or for me. We get weary of doing it all. Some days, you want to throw up your hands and yell, "Lord, why does getting a simple piece of paper or a reply have to be so damn hard!" But there are other moments when I realize what an incredible bond I'm forging with my boys. Yes, as the custodial parent I'm busier and taken for granted at times. Many moms feel this way, yet we find coping strategies.

In Chapter 2, I discussed finding your own therapist to help you sort out matters. I'll add here that joining Parents Without Partners, perhaps the best-known support group for single parents, lends camaraderie. With chapters throughout the United States and Canada, you can reached them at 1-800-637-7974.

Chapter Four

Navigating the Legal Landscape

While the purpose of this book is not to give legal advice or assistance in obtaining the best divorce settlement, it's necessary to navigate the legal system. There are various issues you'll need to address even if you strongly believe you and your husband may eventually reconcile. An attorney can benefit you at each juncture.

How do you find trusted counsel and save money doing so? Is it a good idea for you and your husband to share one attorney? Would it be best to employ a mediator?

In addition, you'll most likely revise your will and change beneficiaries on retirement and other accounts. I'll also discuss taxes, because many legal decisions have tax ramifications. You may even be able to represent yourself on minor matters such as filing a contempt of court motion. And if you plan to remarry, consider a prenuptial agreement.

After reading these pages, you'll hopefully feel more comfortable navigating the legal landscape. In addition, you'll learn to separate the divorce path into the three areas of property division, alimony, and support, as well as child custody.

Should You Call an Attorney?

It's conceivable that you've never before had to hire an attorney, except to write a will. Frankly, it can be upsetting. The day my hands reached for the phone to merely get a referral for a family law attorney, I broke down in tears. I couldn't believe my marriage had come to this.

Like any profession you encounter, there are good attorneys and poor ones. Your job is to weed out the individuals you don't feel comfortable with, those not successful with this type of litigation, and those you simply cannot afford to retain.

Getting over the emotional paralysis of making that first phone call is easier if you look at your initial move as merely a consultation. And indeed that's all you're looking for, in most cases—a free consultation if possible to briefly outline your case. In *Money-Smart Divorce,* Esther Berger writes, "Your first visit to a lawyer will not set in motion anything permanent or irreversible." In fact, she advises that if you ever feel pressured to undertake action you aren't comfortable with, trust your instincts. Voice your concerns. Refuse to sign any agreements before you've had a chance to think. Or, get up and walk out.

Chances are good, however, that you will leave your initial meeting knowing at some level what to do next. It could mean you need other opinions. It could also mean that you feel very satisfied with this attorney's advice, having chosen the lawyer who will see your case to conclusion. Don't be afraid to take notes or ask for language to be clarified in everyday English. You're probably under stress, and that alone impacts your ability to comprehend and listen accurately. But the problem might not be you at all. Avoid any attorney who talks down to you, or anyone you believe is not being completely forthright.

Don't be surprised if your spouse pleads with you *not* to see an attorney. As I've said before, knowledge is power. For whatever reason (and usually selfish ones), your husband may very well be threatened by your moving ahead. I would advise you to get the knowledge and forget his thoughts, for the moment. The same applies if he encourages you to use the same attorney to represent both of you. I honestly don't see how one attorney can look out for both sides.

Very often, the party who seeks legal input first has an edge in the months to come. An initial consultation with someone reassures you. Perhaps your spouse has threatened to sell the house. An attorney can tell you that if the asset is held jointly, your estranged is merely blowing steam.

Your attorney can also warn you about anything that could jeopardize your standing in a subsequent divorce, and give you additional pointers prior to separating. The take-away value of such advice is often substantial, ranging from major moves like bank account transfers or relatively minor details like possessions. For instance, if you really think your future happiness depends upon that brass lamp you got as a wedding gift, best to take it with you in the separation. The same goes for anything of sentimental value, or anything that could be fought over later. And, of course, the children's care should be given great thought. Without a formal custody order, which an attorney can help you with, each parent has equal access to the children. If one shows up to claim them at school or anywhere else, there is little you can do about it without such a document.

Finally, securing an attorney is a step in perhaps the inevitable outcome. As Esther Berger writes, "Divorce is a difficult journey, but for many women it's the road to a much better place."

Selecting an Attorney

Friends or family members who have been pleased by legal services they've received are the best source of referrals. After an initial consultation with one attorney, something inside of me didn't feel right, even though I'd been given great pointers. A family member urged me to seek a second opinion, and I'm glad I did because I ended up with her attorney.

Lacking personal referrals, call your county bar association or look at the National Register of Lawyers. The American Academy of Matrimonial Lawyers in Chicago (312-263-6477) may also refer you to an attorney in your area. Of course, you could also consult the Yellow Pages. It's wiser to use an attorney who regularly practices family law.

Some of the questions you'll want to ask any attorney you interview include:

- What percentage of cases get settled out of court? Do you consider your legal style that of a litigator, negotiator, arbitrator, or mediator?
- How will state laws affect what I'm looking for in custody, support, alimony, and property division?

- Is there a charge for the initial consultation? If so, how much? What is your hourly rate? And are invoices broken down into detail?
- When is a retainer required? What's the amount, and is this money fully refundable in the event it's unused or you do not proceed with any litigation?
- Are there other costs the legal firm bills for, including photocopies, messenger services, etc.?
- Can some research on your case be conducted by paralegal support, which is often less expensive than attorney rates?
- Could your husband be required to pay a portion of your retainer or counsel fees at settlement?

In addition, it's wise to ask during your initial interview some background about the firm and this lawyer's particular experience. For instance, if your case involves domestic violence issues, you'll want someone who truly understands the dynamics of an abusive marriage. Also, how long might your case take? Is it considered complex?

During that initial meeting, you'll need to give a brief summary of what transpired in your marriage that led you to need an attorney. Be as concise as possible. Avoid the "he said, she said" approach. Do not lean on your family law attorney for emotional support. Sure, some handholding might be necessary. But each professional in this world is there to provide a service, and a therapist is much better suited to comfort your emotions than an attorney, whose primary role is to look out for your legal interests. Still, choosing an attorney does involve the personality factor. The two of you should relate well, or you may be better suited to another attorney's style.

Saving Money on Lawyers and Taxes

Usually the cliché refers to death and taxes as being unavoidable, but when you're separated, it may seem like you're dying under a mound of legal expenses instead. It doesn't have to be this way.

For starters, choose an attorney whom you know is fiscally conservative. You find this out from friends or relatives who have used the same counsel. My first attorney slashed several items off my bills because she knew I earned so much less. I was fighting for my children's concerns in many instances, and I think she felt my case was being unnecessarily litigated at various junctures. In other words, she had a heart and a good bedside manner. I hate to say this but there are attorneys who will be adversarial at every opportunity. Sending another nasty letter or taking a matter to court adds to their coffers. This posture doesn't help your sanity, your bank account, or the ongoing relationship you must maintain with your children's father.

In other words, you can control the actions of your attorney by doing proper research in selecting one, and by having some frank money discussions. Realize from the start that most every phone call or meeting with your attorney will cost you, since most attorneys bill in minimum minute increments. That means if you have a five-minute call, you could be charged for fifteen minutes of your attorney's time. Think through your arguments and write down questions before discussing them with your lawyer. I'd often, put my thoughts on paper, review them, and fax them to my attorney.

Of course, when an attorney takes time to read paperwork regarding your case, you'll be billed, even for senseless letters the other side might send. What an utter waste of funds that could be distributed in your settlement or benefit your children!

Whenever you personally gather data, make calls to banks or investment firms, or deal with your estranged spouse to work out minor matters, you do save the cost of an attorney. I estimate that my legal bills through separation and divorce ran between $10,000 to $15,000, for my side alone. In my opinion, at least half of that was completely unnecessary.

With taxes, you'll want to pay close attention to the way court orders are written and designated with regard to alimony and child support payments (see Chapter 6). Typically, the custodial parent receives the tax deduction for minor children. Only when IRS Form 8332 (Release of Claim to Exemption for Child of Divorced or Separated Parents) is signed can the noncustodial parent claim any children as exemptions. You owe it to yourself to run the numbers to determine your tax standing and refund potential before you sign any release forms. Even low-income custodial parents can obtain a refund if they qualify for the earned income credit and file as head of household.

Analyzing your tax position is easily accomplished using TurboTax, MacInTax, or Kiplinger's Tax Cut—all tax preparation products that make preparing and filing your returns less expensive than using a private accountant. Just remember, if you do choose to release the exemption to the other parent, make sure it's only for one tax year, and specify that year on the form. Go through the same analysis for future returns.

Other sound tax moves to consider include taking advantage of the $2,000 IRA deduction if you receive alimony equal to or above that amount. If you receive less than $2,000 in alimony, contribute up to that amount. Even homemakers can qualify for this deduction, and if you can afford in your budget to make the contribution, your future retirement will thank you.

If you are living in the marital residence and maintaining it through support payments, take the mortgage interest deduction if it makes a difference on your taxes. Of course, the standard deduction may at any time be a better move, but the point here is to prevent you from forfeiting this sizeable deduction to an estranged spouse who might hassle to improve his bottom line.

For those women who are self-employed or maybe dream of working from home, realize that there are tax advantages to both. Consult your accountant, and do your research. My book *Working at Home While the Kids Are There, Too* is one place to start.

How you file also deserves some discussion. Some couples file joint returns when they are separated; others wouldn't dream of it. Problem is, until recently, the IRS cracked down rather severely on both spouses, even if one spouse was unaware that the other partner made a mistake, cheated, or simply refused to pay Uncle Sam. Tax reform laws passed in the late 1990s gave some tax relief to the "innocent spouse." But the wronged party still must establish innocence and show that the other spouse was at fault or accrued the tax responsibility. Who wants this additional hassle?

Therefore, think twice before signing a joint return. If you do, make sure the figures are accurate by viewing supporting material (such as W-2s, 1099s, etc.). If there is any doubt as to the return's accuracy, do your own return and check "married, filing separately" or "head of household." When figuring your deductions, plan wisely. Realize that a tax credit is always preferable to a tax deduction because of the effect on your adjusted gross income.

For those women who do file joint returns during their separation, make sure that the refund check gets sent to your accountant or tax preparation office, or better yet, comes to the marital residence you are living in.

Finally, if all this talk of lawyer fees and potential tax liability gets you down, just try to mentally reframe the issue. If you're like me, your personal ad might read some day "Gives good tax return." With several cute exemptions, yourself, and maybe some mortgage interest, you're sure to attract the desire of every bean counter in your community!

Exploring Other Legal Options

You've seen the ads for do-it-yourself divorces, legal clinics, perhaps mediation or arbitration. So are these methods of reaching a divorce settlement beneficial to your cause? The answer: It depends.

First, know that you get what you pay for. According to one family law attorney I consulted, people are often lured by the ads they see in the paper claiming that an attorney can achieve a divorce for them for less than $200. The only problem is that to keep the fees low, these attorneys go off and file for your divorce in another county, where filing fees are significantly less. Sounds good, doesn't it? Until you realize that to litigate any issue you might be driving five hours each way. To transfer the case to your jurisdiction, it costs even more money.

If you are young, married for a relatively short period of time, have few if any assets and no children, you might want to proceed with a do-it-yourself divorce. Your local court can probably give you the necessary paperwork to file, and if you feel you can easily untangle the marital ties that bind you, you would save money. However, this is not the best route for anyone with children, substantial assets, or arguments over alimony (or, really, arguments over anything).

Legal clinics can offer you trained paralegals who have a better knowledge of family law than you might. Again, if you're young, married briefly, have few assets and no children, this could prove beneficial.

Mediation has been discussed in other sections of this book, particularly in regard to child-related matters. But mediating how you'll pick up your children and create a supportive environment is one thing. Mediating a financial settlement and ongoing monetary support is another. Mediation only succeeds when the two of you bring accurate information to the table. If you feel bullied, coerced, or lied to, mediation is senseless. That's why it's ill-advised in abusive marriages. Someone (and usually the husband) has the upper hand, especially in a psychological sense.

Arbitration is another route for avoiding a costly and prolonged legal battle. Here, the arbitrator presides over a minitrial of sorts where the individuals and their attorneys present information. This legal option is sometimes used when the court system is severely backlogged with cases. With arbitration, you can decide in advance whether the arbitrator's decision will be binding or advisory only. And like mediation, you can use arbitration for only some or all aspects of your divorce. In some jurisdictions, the court will approve going to a special master to resolve a particular issue, such as equitable distribution. Your attorney should help you decide if going to a master is your best choice.

Do know that in both mediation, arbitration, and special master options there is no attorney-client privilege. Thus anything you divulge could come out in court.

Whether you choose one of these legal avenues is strictly your choice, but to help you summarize your chances of success, truly consider the level of communication and honesty between you and your estranged husband. If either party operates in a withholding or passive-aggressive mode, your chances for success are slim. Those couples who have realistic requests, no power/control struggles, and the ability to compromise will be much better off. Also know that people who go to court rarely get everything they want. How you proceed is an important decision, to be considered carefully with legal counsel.

Top Ten Legal Mistakes

While many clients have complaints about their lawyers, it's only fair to point out that plenty of attorneys have their lists of factors that make us clients from heaven or hell. According to attorney Karen Myers of the firm Payne Myers in Pittsburgh, calling over and over again just to check in is an utter waste of time and billing.

"Clients ask 'Did you hear anything,'" she says. "If I get word, I'll let you know or send a document I receive out to you in that day's mail." Clients are also advised to seek their legal counsel wisely.

"Telling me 'My friend said this or that, so you're wrong' happens," says Myers, who also cautions people to know the true facts regarding common law marriages in their states. In Pennsylvania, for instance, common law marriage is not automatic just because a couple lives together for seven years. You must prove that you had an informal ceremony or used the same last name. How you filed your taxes matters as well.

Review the blunders we women make as legal clients. You'll be glad you did, and so will your attorney! Here are the top ten legal mistakes I've compiled:

- Believing your spouse will be fair and cooperative. Expect the worst, but allow yourself to be surprised.
- Having totally unrealistic expectations or demands regarding your case.
- Not asking appropriate questions, or signing documents without understanding them.
- Withholding information from your attorney, and/or dumping the entire case in her lap. You should not be a passive participant here.
- Not double-checking facts and figures the other side, or even your attorney, gives you. This includes any invoices from your law firm.
- Allowing emotions rather than logical thinking to rule your legal decisions. Knee-jerk responses are usually inappropriate. Give yourself time to calm down and think first.

- Expecting the legal system to be fair and see things from your perspective.
- Allowing too much time to pass before enforcing a court order or agreed-upon support.
- Forgetting the tax ramifications of legal decisions. That's why having a separate financial advisor or, at the very least, seeing issues from another perspective helps immensely.
- Being a hindrance—not a help—to your case. For instance, it's not wise to annoy your attorney by not paying her or pestering her ad infinitum.

Residency Matters

The state in which you file for divorce (or in which your husband files) is important because each state's laws vary. Some states have no-fault divorce, whereas in others you might file for a more old-fashioned fault divorce based upon grounds (such as adultery, abuse, mental cruelty, addiction, or insanity).

These days no-fault divorce seems to be more popular because parties readily acknowledge incompatibility or an irretrievable breakdown of the marriage. It lessens the need to spy upon or catch a spouse at a particular misdeed. However, there are those who claim that no-fault divorce hurts women who have stood by their marriage and relinquished their careers for their family's nurturance. In some states, fault can only play a factor in certain divorce outcomes (such as awarding alimony). There are those who feel fault should be considered in property division (sometimes called equitable distribution).

The State of Louisiana made news in 1997 as its legislature passed a law enabling couples to opt for a traditional marriage contract or a new covenant contract, aimed at lessening the divorce rate. Couples choosing the covenant marriage have to stay married unless they can prove misconduct such as adultery, abuse, abandonment, or conviction. Before they can divorce, the couple has to be separated for two years unless there is such proof.

That brings us back to the separation stage of a marriage's dissolution. Many states do invoke a waiting period of several months to several years. This is seen as a cooling down period, giving a husband and wife the chance to think seriously about the decision to divorce and change their minds.

A legal annulment of your marriage is always an option if you meet your state's criteria. This court action voids your marriage as if it did not take place. (This is separate from a religious annulment.) Annulments aren't as common today since the social stigma of divorce barely exists. Check your state's laws, but an annulment may apply if your spouse lied to you or misled you in some way (perhaps you want a family but your husband cannot have children, or even worse, he's already married), your spouse isn't of legal age, you were forced to marry, or you were under the influence of drugs or alcohol when tying the knot. While an annulment might legally void your marriage, it will not change your responsibilities to any children resulting from your relationship.

A default divorce can sometimes be granted if you cannot find your estranged husband. In most states, you file for divorce, publish a legal notice that you are doing so, and if your spouse fails to respond, you can be granted a divorce by default after a particular length of time.

The bottom line here is to carefully consider the state in which you'll proceed with a divorce. Though you've undoubtedly heard of the quick celebrity divorces, most states maintain a residency requirement. And as I said in the first chapter, look with suspicion to any husband who wants to move abruptly when the marriage is plummeting. He could be trying to move to a state that would grant a divorce more to his liking.

In addition, the county in which you proceed matters a great deal. For instance, two adjacent counties may have different laws. Technically, you can file for a divorce in the county either party resides in, or the county of the marital residence. But if one county allows you to bifurcate the divorce more easily (grant the divorce first, the property division later), this is a substantial consideration. Women generally do not want to bifurcate because doing so often means they will cease medical insurance coverage and other benefits from their husband.

Legal vs. Informal Separations

Some states have what is called a legal separation. If this is the case, you may want to file a petition for separation with your family court. After you've worked out the terms, the agreement is also filed with the court. That's why it is wise to consult an attorney to ascertain your state's laws even in regard to separation. There have been instances where one party walks out in a fit of rage only to discover later she's jeopardized her claim to the marital residence, many of the possessions, perhaps even primary custody of the children.

A formal separation agreement can address any issues you'd like spelled out on paper. Some items include who will stay in the house, how you will share your joint assets, who will have custody and care for the children (or visitation times), alimony and child support, and other expenses, such as health care. It's wise to include mention of debt and credit, for if one spouse mismanages the money or racks up joint debt, your credit history will be damaged. (Chapter 6 goes into greater detail.) Someone will have to pay off any joint debt you already owe. Stipulate that your spouse will not include your name on any new credit cards, debts, or bank accounts—that he must not sign your name to *anything* without your written consent.

If your state allows for a legal separation and your communication is so destroyed that you cannot cooperate, entering into a formal agreement is wise. Without such a document, you can't ask the court to enforce it should even the most amicable relationship turn sour. And if you reconcile, great. Providing your agreement doesn't need to be withdrawn from court, simply file it away or tear it up.

When your state does not recognize a legal separation, you can informally separate. Provided you both can support yourselves, you have no minor children together, nor any joint assets, you might get by without much legal intervention. But if these criteria do not apply, or if you simply cannot cooperate or communicate, it's best to put things in writing.

Preparing Your Case

If you want a crash course on the various phases of divorce litigation, *Divorce For Dummies* by John Ventura and Mary Reed steps you through the terminology and process you're likely to travel. Again, this is assuming you don't settle out of court. For many reasons it's wise to avoid court whenever possible. It's expensive, mentally draining, and often unsatisfactory in the results it yields. According to these authors, only about 5 percent of all divorces are settled inside a courtroom.

Nonetheless, Ventura and Reed discuss pretrial motions, the process of discovery, interrogatories, pretrial conferences, and hearings with a judge. Your attorney will be your ultimate guide, but in the interest of time and money, becoming familiar with the legal procedures on your own can only help you.

Depending upon the complexity of your case, if you go to trial, be forewarned of the expense, not only for your own attorney's counsel but also for filing fees, court reporters, expert witnesses, subpoenas, exhibits, and miscellaneous fees, all of which add up to a substantial bill.

Of course, if you read the advice I gave in the first chapter, you know how important it is to have the documents and paper trails you need to prove your claim on various assets, or even prove that these assets exist. Nothing will help you obtain a favorable settlement like good sleuth work, organization, and being prepared.

Having Your Day in Court

Yes, everyone talks about having her day in court. In most cases, however, you are better off trying to reach a settlement outside of formal litigation before a judge. You might even reach such agreement on the proverbial courthouse steps. It happens all the time.

However, there may be issues where you must appear before a hearing officer or judge. On those occasions, it's best to follow some guidelines.

For starters, be prepared and appear on time. Dress neatly and conservatively. You don't want to wear flashy clothing or expensive jewelry, nor do you want to appear poverty-stricken. Show respect by not chewing gum, smoking, swearing, or acting overly angry or even flippant. If you must display an emotion, crying is better than most of your other choices. Indeed, if you act too out of line, you may be held in contempt of court for your actions.

Make sure you understand any questions posed to you. If they are unclear, ask politely if the question could be repeated. In addition, learn to rein in your responses. In court, less is more. So refrain from telling your life story. Answer only what you must and do so as concisely as possible.

Be courteous. "Yes, Your Honor" or "thank you, Attorney Smith" goes a long way in creating favorable impressions. If you want to communicate with your lawyer prior to a recess, scrawl a note on a piece of paper. But do not interrupt or blurt out your thoughts. This is inappropriate and distracting while your attorney tries to focus on your case at hand.

Sure, you'll be uneasy and perhaps upset during court appearances, particularly if you are charged with doing or saying things that never occurred. Take a friend to wait outside for moral support and be with you on the way into and from court that day. I know one woman who kept a small photo of her son in her pocket during cross-examination. And when I represented myself on a few issues, one of my best friends offered to go with me for moral support.

Of course, if your case is decided in court, you may not be pleased with the outcome. You can appeal a judge's decision, but appeals on divorces aren't always easy to win. The biggest issue you may want to consider is cost to your pocketbook and sanity. Keeping up the fight is draining to all parties involved, and it does filter down to the children. In some cases, the amount of money you'll spend to fight the decision will impede other goals (such as hanging on to your house or completing your education).

Furthermore, an appeal may not be heard for many months, and then you face yet another trial. Living in this kind of legal limbo is not pleasant, and in essence prevents you from obtaining the emotional divorce you need to get on with your life. The appeal process may force you to switch attorneys if your present lawyer doesn't feel confident he or she can win the case. You also have no guarantee that a new judge will rule any more to your liking than the first. A faster and less expensive way to appeal particular aspects of your case could be through modification, legalese for a change (such as with custody or support issues petitioned separately).

Representing Yourself on Minor Issues

When does it make sense to ask your attorney to withdraw and represent yourself on minor issues? Well, there is no easy answer. During a separation most couples encounter a variety of issues that warrant an attorney's intervention, advice, and services. So I am not going to tell you to ask your attorney to formally withdraw from your case prematurely.

But if you're like me, there comes a point when you are weary of lawyers and their fees. Indeed, some estranged or ex-husbands see the legal system as a toy or weapon they can use to vent their anger. They might know, for instance, that every time their lawyer writes a nasty gram to your attorney, you might choose to ignore the contents, but indeed you'll be billed for the time taken to read and forward the letter to you. If one party is in a more secure financial position and vindictive enough, this can become another form of abuse, in the legal and financial realm.

Thus, during your separation, I'd hang on to your attorney but choose your battles wisely. Every letter you receive doesn't require a response. Indeed if you dash off a reply, you're fueling the flames of anger, which might be exactly what your estranged husband had in mind. Why give him the satisfaction? (It might just tick him off more if you ignore the issue, and you'll certainly be less in debt to your legal firm.) However, there will come a day when your case reaches a settlement, and at that juncture or shortly thereafter, you may want your attorney to withdraw.

Sure, there might still be squabbles. But an ordinary mortal can present a motion in court. If you aren't an assertive and communicative type, this might not be the best strategy for you. Knowing my own nature, I gave it a try when I needed to enforce an issue to reach closure in my divorce settlement. I figured if I could write ninety-five-thousand-word books, I could darn well draft a simple motion following the format of so many I had in my files.

When you represent yourself in court it is considered pro se representation. People do this in small claims court all the time. In the case of family law, it might make sense to go to court pro se over an issue of minor expenses due you or for a form that needs to be signed. For instance, if your ex-husband owes you approximately $100 in unreimbursed medical expenses, you could conceivably spend more in attorney's fees than the ultimate amount of the reimbursement. To my mode of thinking, that's senseless. Some pro se motions courts offer free legal assistance depending upon income.

Considering that you might choose a pro se court action at some juncture, do hang on to prior motions and drafted court orders when you begin weeding out your files. Keep these merely to follow the format if you must write a motion yourself. If there is one judge assigned to your case, you'll want to bring the matter before his or her attention. To find out the court schedule of when particular judges will hear motions that month, look at a copy of your county legal journal in the library. You might know a kind-hearted attorney friend who could give you the information and dates you need, or you could call the judge's secretary, stating that you have a pro se motion to present and would like to know when Judge Smith is hearing motions.

If you have a few items to discuss, the judge may slate your case for a judicial conference where the parties (and attorneys if there are any) meet with the judge a little more informally, reviewing unresolved issues and receiving the judge's take on the matters involved. This one meeting might be enough to get one or both of you to budge, cooperate, and settle the dispute.

Any time you go to court, follow the guidance in this chapter regarding dress and your demeanor. Gather your paperwork in an organized manner. If you write a motion, you can photocopy particular evidence and label these as exhibits. It's always best to be more prepared than less.

Preparing a Prenuptial Agreement

If you plan to remarry down the road, it's wise to review your entire estate plan and draft a prenuptial agreement. I have friends who say they could never entertain the thought. Where's the trust, they say? If you have gained assets, and particularly if there are children involved, you *must* look out for their interests as well as yours. That's your job. This isn't about love, or lack of it. It's about basic responsibility.

Drafting a prenup calms many people's fears—your own, your intended's, and those of children from previous marriages. It merely states that what has been yours will remain as yours. This alone is important. In cases of considerable wealth or inheritances, this is even more appropriate. It just does not make good sense following a divorce to co-mingle all of your assets. If you've worked hard to build a portfolio for yourself, keep it that way. Limit what you jointly title or share at the bank.

At least six months before your remarriage, hire separate attorneys to draft an agreement and sign it. The more distance you can put between signing the document and walking down the aisle, the better. This also allows you to enjoy the excitement of planning your nuptials more fully. Furthermore, if you sign under pressure (i.e., on the way to the altar) the agreement may be rendered null and void if ever disputed. That's why some attorneys videotape their clients signing the document to have as evidence that neither was coerced.

Don't underestimate what you own. Take time to list everything that's important to you and your children, including those personal belongings you wish for them to have someday. The added perk here is having a complete inventory for insurance purposes should you ever need to make claims on account of fire, theft, or other disasters.

Of course, pre nup agreements can go into greater detail. They can discuss what expenses will be shared during the marriage or how much alimony one of you would receive upon another divorce. They can also outline how you live, how much debt you'll take on, how many children you want and how soon, who will share the housework, and who makes decisions. In my opinion, outlining the disposition of certain assets and agreeing to be compensated for one party's contribution to higher education is one thing. Spelling out where you'll spend holidays and day-to-day decisions is a bit restrictive. But to each his own, as they say.

For more information regarding prenups, read *How to Write Your Own Premarital Agreement* by Edward A. Haman. *Divorce For Dummies,* already listed in this chapter, has useful information on prenuptial agreements as well. Even if you draft your own agreement, it's wise to seek legal counsel to make sure it's notarized and binding.

Chapter Five

Preserving Your Personal Safety

A marital separation can be a volatile time. If you've seen any data from stress questionnaires, you'll notice that it ranks up there under death of a spouse. That stress sometimes causes people to act impulsively, without thought to consequences, and with retribution in mind.

For all of these reasons, this chapter is devoted to ensuring your personal safety, and the protection of your children and your property. It will also deal with preserving your sanity if there is emotional abuse, stalking, and harassment.

I'm not trying to alarm you with instructions to secure your house like Fort Knox or to take precautions you might term extreme. However, in cases where there has been domestic violence, a woman is most vulnerable to attack (emotional or physical) when she tries to break away and establish a new life.

Even if you feel you have not experienced abuse, still read this chapter. You'll become familiar with patterns of abusive behavior and know exactly how to protect yourself if you feel sufficiently threatened. Besides, now that you are living alone, there are safety measures that any woman can benefit from learning.

What Is Domestic Violence?

So often we view domestic violence solely as physical assault. For many years in my marriage, things didn't seem right. No, I never ended up in an emergency room. But I felt threatened, terrorized by certain actions, and abused by words and behaviors. It wasn't until I sought individual therapy and counseling at a women's shelter that I came to terms with the fact that I, too, was a victim.

Domestic abuse knows no boundaries. It occurs without regard to race, religion, income, profession, neighborhood, or social status. Second, domestic violence encompasses the following:

> **Physical abuse** is hitting, pushing, shoving, kicking, slapping, burning, and choking. It involves objects or weapons intended to cause injury, and it includes physical force that might prevent you from leaving home or fleeing an attack.

> **Mental abuse** includes telling you what you can and can't do, calling you names, using foul language and words that hurt, threatening you, or belittling you in verbal assaults. This type of abuse also includes

withholding postures, the persistent use of passive aggression, and manipulation.

Sexual abuse is identified as rape, forcing you to perform particular sexual activities against your will, or touching you in a manner you deem inappropriate or unpleasant.

Property and economic abuse entails stealing or destroying personal belongings, even if those belongings were marital property. Examples include kicking doors, breaking windows, and smashing your favorite antique vase. It includes hurting pets, withholding money, or refusing to meet needs for shelter, food, and clothing.

Having read these descriptions, many of us could recognize a time in our own behavior when perhaps we called someone a name in an argument or threw the newspaper down at the end of a rough day. It's the persistent pattern of poor behavior that makes it abuse. In many cases, emotional abuse is the precursor for physical violence and property destruction. When a man kicks in a door or hurls a glass vase, the woman thinks she's next.

One minute your husband is calm, the next he's raging. In cases like these, a wife becomes the lightening rod for all the emotional storms in her husband's life. He might be able to change this pattern of behavior, but he might not. Domestic violence is never the victim's fault. The responsibility for behaving nonviolently is an individual one. Bottom line: There is no excuse for abuse.

I compiled the list of abusive behaviors after much research. Looking over that list, there isn't a doubt in my mind that I sought the right kind of counseling for me and my two sons. But the good news is that I'm a survivor, and you can be one also. No one—I repeat, *no one*—deserves to be abused.

Control Issues and Crazymaking

The mistreatment of a woman by a man with whom she lives or has had a romantic relationship is an attempt to gain and maintain control over her. Such power is exerted through physical force, terroristic behavior, economic deprivation, and sexual abuse. In a subtler sense, control manifests itself through withholding, countering, blocking, diverting, and blaming. Sure we all do one of these things from time to time, but an abuser uses whatever methods he can to perpetuate a cycle of oppression and control.

Donald G. Dutton, Ph.D., a professor of psychology at the University of British Columbia, has written books on domestic abuse and has served as an expert witness in prominent legal cases, including the O. J. Simpson trial. He writes that when we try to control something, there is usually anxiety or anger.

Suffice to say these men are dealing with larger problems. An abuser becomes skillful at projecting negative traits onto his partner such as finding a fault in her that indeed he perceives in himself. Have you ever wondered if your partner is actually two people? The public persona who gets along with others, and the private man who only rages in the intimate relationship?

I came to the conclusion in my own life that it didn't quite matter what I did. Something would spark resentment or anger. I couldn't win for losing. I remember planning a vacation to an island we'd both dreamed of visiting. I took both our hobbies into account. We'd saved for this trip, and I had checked with my husband before making reservations. Closer to departure, I got the impression that I was perceived as "controlling" for making these plans.

This type of crazymaking, as author Patricia Evans calls it, is a way of life for some. "If your partner seems irritated or angry at you several times a week; denies being angry when he clearly is; does not work with you to resolve important issues; rarely or never seems to share thoughts or plans with you; or tells you he has no idea what you're talking about when you try to discuss important problems, you need my book," says Evans.

"Whether control is exercised verbally or physically, the dynamics are the same," she writes in *The Verbally Abusive Relationship.* It all revolves around oppression and control. A raised fist, a push, or an unspoken threat like punching the wall leaves a woman in fear of her partner for a long time to come. "Of course, when this occurs," Evans writes, "the relationship is definitely one of oppression."

Review the signs of abuse in this chapter and really think about your husband's behavior. It might even be wise to run the list by a trusted friend who has seen you and your partner interact. Sometimes a third party can be more objective, recognizing things we remain blind to.

Dealing with Verbal Intimidation

When a woman faces the dissolution of her marriage, it's more the rule these days than the exception that she will endure a tirade of remarks to convince her to reconcile or to intimidate her during the litigation process. Often these remarks come from her estranged husband. Be prepared to hear such remarks as these:

- I'm going to drag this case out forever. You'll get nothing.
- I'm going to file for custody and take the children from you.
- I've got a pitbull lawyer who will eat you alive.
- Your attorney is a crook out for every last dime.
- I was going to give you a fair settlement. But you went and got yourself an attorney (moved out, got a restraining order, etc.), so now forget it.
- I'll tell our children how terrible you are, and they'll never love you.
- If you don't settle this case fast, I'll drag your boyfriend (family, friends) into this case and make all of you miserable.

When faced with such a nasty litany, remember that when people aim to control with harsh words, they are indeed the ones with the fear and anger. Your best defense is to ignore the remarks. Sure, they hurt. Sure, you should look out for your legal interests and protect yourself in every way. But words are words. Just because they are uttered does not mean they will impact your life.

As a woman and a wife, you have every right to demand respect from your partner, even when you are separated. If there is any possibility of a reconciliation, you should not have to endure the silent treatment, stored grudges, or unfinished arguments handled in anything less than civil discussion. You should expect heartfelt apologies when called for (but do read about contrition below). Even if divorce is imminent, never tolerate abuse—whether it involves physical, emotional, or verbal battering.

"A good man will generally treat a woman the way she demands to be treated," says Mary E. O'Brien, M.D."If a man will hit you once, he'll eventually hit you again, no matter how passionately he pleads forgiveness." I think the same can be said of verbal intimidation. If he feels he can accomplish something with senseless remarks or nasty letters from his attorney, he has no incentive to stop.

Signs of Abusive Behavior

No woman pictures herself with an abusive partner. All too often, she was swept off her feet by a man whose complex behavior unveiled itself as time went on. Use the following list to tell if your husband has abusive characteristics. Having one or two traits does not make him abusive. However, if you spot several, discuss your thoughts with a counselor.

- **Do you see signs of controlling behavior?** Abuse is about the struggle for power. A man who interrogates you about where you were or sets limits over whom you can interact with and when you have time to yourself is high on control issues.

- **Were you pressured for a quick commitment?** Abusers prey on weak women, those ending another relationship or otherwise vulnerable. Did you have little time to get to know your partner? Beware if a man who just ended a relationship comes courting you.
- **Does he exhibit signs of jealous rage?** If you're made to feel bad about talking with another man, accused of flirting, or called nasty names that imply you're unfaithful, there's jealousy. And if your husband follows you, monitors your phone calls, or has fits of anger, there is a serious problem. Love is not isolation.
- **Is he the blaming kind?** Abusive men are savvy at turning the blame around to partners, manipulating feelings to make it seem that they are the victims, that they have been harmed. It's crazymaking. You'll rarely find an abuser who accepts responsibility. Abusers shirk it. Remember, there is no excuse for abuse.
- **Have you been verbally abused?** Cruel and hurtful remarks are never called for. And it's a sad fact that a great deal of domestic violence begins with verbal and emotional battering.
- **Does your man use physical force?** Whether it's destroying property, blocking your exit, raising fists, pushing, threatening to harm, demanding sexual compliance, or actually assaulting you, it's not right. Force is frequently a means to manipulate and control.
- **Do you see a pattern of contrition?** Do you see a pattern of acting out, then a remorseful stage in which

you're promised it will never happen again? Well, it usually does happen again, only with more severity. Promises rarely work, and flowers won't fix it. Explosive mood swings deserve medical and mental health care, before your well-being suffers further.

- **Has anyone reported episodes of previous battering?** If someone in this man's past (a former girlfriend, an ex-wife, or a child) has reported being battered, listen with both ears. He isn't going to own up to his responsibility. He'll only justify and rationalize his behavior.

Legal Protection from Abuse

If you're a victim of domestic violence, you can choose to end the struggle and begin a better life. Police forces across the country are becoming more aware of domestic abuse, for it is a crime. For instance, they can arrest your husband or ask him to leave. Many police departments have informational sheets to leave with women, instructing them how to file for a restraining order (a protection from abuse order).

If you find yourself sufficiently threatened, do file for a protective order. There is no guarantee that your estranged husband won't violate it, but if he does, the law is definitely on your side. Such an order will keep him away from your home, job, or school and forbid him from assaulting, threatening, harassing, or stalking you. It may also provide protection to your children.

Protective orders can spell out exactly what an abusive man can and cannot do, and indeed what he is required to do (such as pay interim support, enter a counseling program, refrain from drugs or alcohol, or have supervised visitation with his children). Temporary or emergency orders are granted for approximately seventy-two hours, and remain in effect until you can appear before a judge for an extended order.

Truly, you can get this kind of emergency protection at any time of the day or night. District magistrates often hear cases, or you may petition in night court. You do *not* need an attorney (though taking a friend for emotional support is a good idea). If granted, you'll be given duplicate copies of the court order. Take these to the police, who will need to serve your estranged husband with the order. They keep a copy, and you keep a copy for your records.

Once you have a temporary order, it's wise to consult an attorney on how to proceed for further protection. If you cannot afford counsel, there is often free legal aid rendered to battered women regardless of income. Most counties provide this help. Knowing your rights is another reason to consult a shelter. To find one near you, call the National Domestic Violence Hotline at 1-800-799-SAFE (7233). And to learn more about legal protection you can read *What To Do When Love Turns Violent* by Marian Betancourt.

Battered Woman Syndrome

Why didn't you just leave? It's always the first question people wonder. If you're the woman, perhaps you wondered why on earth you've stayed in a poor relationship.

But a woman who has been abused is running on empty with little self-esteem, and has a shattered concept of her place in the world, few resources including money, and perhaps a deficit of job skills. Frequently, battering escalates at times when a woman is most vulnerable, including during pregnancy.

The battered woman forgives, she hopes, she continues to love, until she's so confused that the next cycle occurs. The battering escalates. It explodes. There's the honeymoon period again. Over and over again.

Lenore Walker presented her groundbreaking research in 1979 in *The Battered Woman* in terms of the tension-building phase leading to the explosion (the battering incident), and ending with contrition (professing love, sending flowers, promising the abuse will never happen again).

The good news is that recovery is your right. A battered woman's best chance of escaping abuse is to get herself appropriate counseling as quickly as possible.

Counseling and Recovery

For me, education was key in breaking away from a poor relationship. Fortunately, I'm an avid reader. Once I began reading about domestic violence and the patterns of abuse, I didn't feel as overwhelmed. In their book *When Men Batter Women,* Neil Jacobson, Ph.D. and John Gottman, Ph.D. make a good case against seeking marriage counseling to remedy abuse. First, they suggest, marital therapy puts the couple together more frequently where they are encouraged to deal with conflict. And if the couple is treated together, it's implied that each party is responsible for the problems. This is sure handy for your husband if he's abusive since it supports his point of view.

So what kind of counseling should you seek? Your own. Cognitive therapy will help you adjust thinking patterns that became unhealthy and may have led you to put up with poor treatment.

Outside of psychotherapy, you'll find that advocates and counselors at your local women's shelter are very helpful. It's a big step to call a shelter for help, let alone walk through the doors for an appointment. But I've been there. I'm so glad I sought that kind of support because I realized I wasn't alone.

There is a wonderful life of peace and happiness out there for you. In time, the wounds of mistreatment and violence will heal. The sooner you seek help, the quicker you will recover.

How Abuse Affects Children

Children who witness violence early in life come to see the world as a dangerous, unpredictable, and unloving place. Some researchers have found that many children exposed to the trauma of violence develop psychiatric problems later in life. Girls who routinely see their mothers abused fall into the same scenarios. And truly, those boys who grow up with a battering role model may know of no other way to solve problems with their own wives.

Some of the behaviors you might recognize in children exposed to domestic abuse include poor impulse control, externalizing or internalizing of anger, sadness, depression, stress, and school delinquency. These children are at higher risk and may act out with drugs, alcohol, and sex. They may even blame themselves for not being able to prevent abuse to their mothers.

But your children don't have to suffer. Many women's centers and shelters offer pro bono children's programs with trained counselors or group activities. Through the intervention of a shelter program, children can see males standing up against violence as well, and they can learn to be proud of their mothers for being strong.

By going to a group session with their peers, trained counselors, and volunteers, boys and girls will learn that they are not alone. Often, children feel singled out in a separated or divorcing family, especially if the other children they associate with come from intact homes. Add the component of being from an abusive home, and it merely compounds the loneliness. Help is available, and you owe it to your children to seek out such assistance. A pattern of abuse that may have lasted through generations can end.

After at least a year attending the pro bono children's program at our local women's shelter, my son and I were reading books about his new pet, a hermit crab named Freddie. We learned that when you have multiple crabs sharing the same environment, it's not uncommon that one fights the other to obtain custody of the shell. My son, who was eight at the time, got quiet for a moment.

"You know, mom," he said. "If we get another crab and it's a girl, Freddie could get arrested for doing that."

In one brief moment, I realized how much my son had already learned about the appropriate and inappropriate ways of treating women. "Praise God," I wanted to proclaim. The effort of driving to the shelter and back each week really did pay off! If you find that your children, particularly sons, are troubled by what they have witnessed, or are hitting or verbally battering you, seek counseling for them right away.

State legislatures are also recognizing the effects of domestic violence on children, and many are passing laws that make it more difficult for the batterer to obtain custody. It's advisable that you inform your pediatrician and any other relevant professional in your child's life about the domestic violence in your marriage, whether it was witnessed or not. This can become a part of their records that can help others understand how to help your child, and it may strengthen your case if there are future custody battles.

Finally, know that many shelters have an age range for the children that they accept, particularly boys. Sometimes, boys over age thirteen or fourteen cannot live with their mothers in shelter accommodations. If you feel you need a shelter stay, it's better to make this move when your son is ten than wait until your options are limited.

Keeping Safe

Victims of domestic violence need to take added precautions to ensure their safety. Often dubbed developing an escape plan, it's advisable to keep an extra set of keys, clothing, important papers, prescriptions, and some cash or credit cards with someone you trust. Identify a safe place for children to go during intense conflict, assuring them of their role to be safe, not to protect you.

Call the police. Have the numbers of friends, family, and your nearest shelter available to you at all times. Arrange a secret distress signal with neighbors so that they can summon help if you can't. If you're injured, go to the emergency room, where physicians are trained to help you report and heal from your ordeal. Do not leave the hospital without a safety plan that's known only to friends and family.

Safety Measures and the Children

Up to 75 percent of all reported domestic violence assaults take place after parents have separated, with the highest risk involving the transfer of the couple's children, according to a study published in 1992 in the *Juvenile and Family Court Journal.* Be extra-vigilant during exchanges.

Also, teach your children good safety habits. They should know, if they are old enough, what their regular and scheduled visitation times are with their fathers. This way, if they are approached by the parent at another time, they will know first-hand where they are to be. Think your estranged husband wouldn't lure his own children away? Guess again.

Give copies of protective orders or your custody agreement to your children's school, youth group, scoutmaster, day-care center, doorman, or building manager. This way, if your estranged husband tries to take the children at times visitation is not specified, others will know not to release them to him.

And, teach children emergency contact numbers, such as your phone number, a relative's number, or the police/emergency number just in case they are left alone. As one mom who had a belligerent spouse put it, "Most kids ponder what clothes to wear, but our kids have to be prepared to be Columbo detectives." The kids' father got angry and left them stranded at a restaurant. Fortunately, these children knew what to do.

Securing Your Household

If you think abuse is likely, file for exclusive possession of your home. This helps when your spouse lords it over you that the house belongs to him as well. In situations where he shows up in a rage, the police can make him leave if you have exclusive possession of the marital residence.

Often, exclusive possession is granted as part of a protective or restraining order. But it can be placed into any agreements you devise with your estranged spouse. As I indicated before, visitation exchanges are often fraught with discord. Specify in your custody order, for instance, that the children's father is to remain in the car at all times. Or you can designate another, neutral location to exchange the children. Popular sites include your local police station or even within the court house—both places where there is surveillance.

But remember, an agreement is only a piece of paper. Your best bet is to remain cautious. Nasty behavior occurs when you least expect it. One woman reported that she and her husband had an agreement that he let their children into the house, staying until she arrived. Weeks later, after one of her estranged husband's drop-offs, this woman reached into the wine cellar for a bottle to serve to guests. Only then did she discover that hundreds of dollars of wine had been literally poured down the drain. The note left behind stated, "You don't need to be drinking this."

Honestly, I can't understand why an estranged husband should ever have access to your home after you have separated. At the very least, there should be others present, besides you and the children. Such entries only bring on remarks about new possessions and changes you've made, or even roaming eyes that may be casing the place.

Beyond obtaining exclusive possession, here is a checklist of home security measures all women should take when separated:

- Change the locks if you aren't certain you have all his keys to the property. If he has a key to get in, he will most likely pay you a visit when you are not home, and take any number of possessions and documents. Don't think he'd do that? It is not worth taking the chance. It happens in the majority of marital separations. In some communities, if you have a protective order, you might be eligible for assistance in changing your locks.
- If you don't have deadbolt locks, install these along with chains on all outside doors. Steel doors are always better than wooden doors or those with glass panels that can be broken to gain access.
- Install a security system in the residence, or change any access codes. Don't forget about garage door access. Retrieve his remote control device and/or the garage door key. Reprogram this entry if necessary.
- Retrieve any hidden keys that you stuck under doormats or under rocks in the bushes in case of emergency. Don't forget about keys that might remain with friends or family. (If his family members or friends have keys, you must re-key the locks).
- Consider that kids and keys might not mix well, at least for a while. You don't want your ex to take a key belonging to your children. There isn't an easy solution to your children's access to your home. Until you've been granted exclusive possession or the marital residence is deeded to you in a divorce, the police can do little if your estranged husband shows up with a key, presuming the property is jointly held. If at all possible,

try to keep the keys to yourself, and ask trusted adults to let children inside.

- Instruct children that nothing leaves the house to go to dad's without your permission. Sometimes the kids are asked to retrieve objects that estranged husbands feel entitled to.
- Inform neighbors of your situation. As embarrassing as it may seem, they will most likely be helpful and understanding. Neighbors are wonderful watchdogs, especially if they are at home during the day or are the vigilant type. Instruct them to call the police if they see your estranged on the premises when you aren't there to handle the situation (or any time if there's been a history of violence). Of course, they should never permit access to your residence by giving a key you might leave with them for emergencies.
- Keep a cellular phone handy for emergencies. Whether in your house or on the highway, a mobile phone works when lines have been severed or if you are not near a regular telephone.
- If you experience telephone harassment, consult your telephone company. In fact, your telephone directory might step you through how to report such pranks, but in some cases if you proceed with the instructions, then you must also be willing to prosecute. After you hang up with a harasser, pick the phone back up and press *57 (or dial 1157). This reports and traces it.
- Set your answering machine to record all incoming calls. This can also deter telephone harassment. Keep a

supply of extra tapes on hand so that you can save any messages of a harassing nature.

- Since many answering machines have remote access to messages when you're away from home, invest in a new answering system. You don't want your estranged husband to listen to any messages or information conveyed confidentially to you. Never leave a message on your machine that you are away.

Other Home Security Measures

Your security measures will depend largely upon where you live. For instance, if you are in an urban or perhaps high-crime neighborhood, you might want to install grates or grilles on outdoor windows. Make sure that window air conditioners are properly secured. Sliding glass doors should be locked at the handle, secured at the top (with a latch you can purchase), and additionally protected with a piece of wood fit to the space between the frame and the inside panel.

If you have outdoor landscaping, prune any tree limbs that could allow a burglar's access to the second story, and trim shrubbery so that doors and windows are visible. Lock up any ladders you leave outdoors, and think twice about high wooden fences. These, like shrubbery, make it easy for criminals to hide.

You can purchase window stickers and signs at home building centers that warn intruders of electronic surveillance systems. In addition, you can purchase or borrow electric engraving pens to mark all items that would-be thieves (or your estranged spouse) might take. These include all stereo, television, video, camera or computer equipment, expensive appliances, or anything else of value. Make a video of your household contents (including china, silver, and jewelry), and store this record of your belongings in your safe deposit box. You'll be better able to identify what you have (and it's a handy tool for filing insurance claims as well).

Hire house-sitters for funerals or celebrations when others might know you aren't home. Tell the police of your vacation so that they can enter you into their log book. Stop deliveries, and ask the neighbors to pick up any items left on your doorstep. Give your home a lived-in look by putting lights on timers, having the lawn mowed, and even asking neighbors to leave footprints or their cars in your driveway. Have them report any suspicious persons seen hanging around.

Personal Safety in General

Now that you are separated, you increase the chances that you'll be traveling on your own, not only on the highways but around the community and out of town.

Again, common sense dictates that you plan personal or business errands in daylight, that you travel with a friend, and that you don't drive or walk through the more dangerous parts of town. But crime can happen anywhere, at any time of the day.

Some women feel safer if they have pepper spray (mace is illegal in some areas), a personal alarm (available at home supply centers), or a pendant alarm (given by some police departments to victims of domestic violence). These are added measures, but only if you use them or have them at the ready.

The best advice when traveling alone is to be vigilant. Know your surroundings. Keep an eye on others. Walk confidently and quickly to your car or destination. Don't limit your mobility with heavy packages or luggage.

When traveling away from home, insist on hotel security. Clerks should hand you your room key and number silently. If your accommodations do not seem secure, ask for a room change. Mark your luggage with just a first initial, last name, and office address if possible (or post office box). Don't be fooled by uniforms, either. Always ask for proper identification before admitting anyone to a hotel room or home, or even rolling down your car window.

A good resource for you to peruse is *A Woman's Guide To Personal Safety* by Janeé Harteau and Holly Keegel. You'll learn precautions to take that you may not have thought applied to you.

A Word about Firearms

When women are concerned about personal safety, they might be tempted to purchase a weapon, usually a gun, for their protection. But it's paramount that you receive proper training, and if you own firearms of any kind, that you keep them unloaded and locked away from children's reach (even teenagers).

The mere need to lock away protection and ammunition might deter you from ownership in the first place. If there was an intruder, it would take time to get to such a weapon. But your children's safety comes first here, as well as your own. Guns owned by the inexperienced are frequently confiscated by criminals and used against the owners.

Even for those women who don't have kids around, do seek proper training if you choose to buy a gun. One of my friend's husband offered to take me to a local sportsmen's club to learn to handle a gun safely at the shooting range. Check with friends who have experience with firearms and ask how they learned to use a weapon safely. If you don't have anyone to ask, call your local police department for class referrals. Police departments also have literature on storing guns safely, and officers frequently lecture in schools and in the community.

Maintaining Confidentiality

We live in a technological world in which anyone can obtain access to privileged information. If you don't use caution, that anyone could even be your estranged spouse finding out information you'd rather keep to yourself.

For instance, did you know that anyone can look up your posts to Internet newsgroups merely by doing a search with the right web site? That's right. It's great to find new cyberfriends and share online, but never divulge information you wouldn't want discovered. When you are litigating a legal separation or divorce case, you never know what could be used against you (such as job information, successes, personal struggles, etc.).

If you truly want to keep your address and whereabouts confidential, refrain from any deliveries, including newspapers, even pizza. Get a post office box and use that for mail. In fact, make sure the post office knows that your estranged husband has no business picking up mail or packages that might be held for you. When you travel out of town, or even are away for a day, have your mail held at the post office or ask a trusted neighbor to retrieve it. After all, you don't want your estranged spouse taking documents out of the mailbox.

Similarly, change your passwords or make them less obvious to others. These include passwords to your computer, e-mail account, ATM, or even utilities. Yes, without your knowledge, your telephone service could be altered unless you have protected your account with a password. Representatives will ask you for the magic word each time you make a change in service.

Victims of domestic violence should also inquire about getting a new social security number assigned to them if it's warranted. Contact the Social Security office near you, or ask for assistance with this at your local women's shelter. Too much information in the wrong hands is a bad thing.

Finally, having an unlisted phone number is advisable for many reasons, security being chief among them. Realize also that if your estranged spouse has caller ID, your number might be displayed unless you block it in advance. To do this, press *67 (or dialing 1167) before entering the phone number. Line blocking, available through the phone company, might be another option.

The best deterrent to crime, or even harassment, is prevention. This chapter was not meant to alarm you, but to prepare you for an easier way of life that is not complicated by anything unforeseen happening. It's a good idea to review safety measures periodically since we all get busy and push prevention aside. If the ideas presented here make you feel more secure, or indeed prevent unfortunate occurrences, then this chapter has served its purpose.

Chapter Six

Your Financial Future

Immediate money matters plague many separated women. Some are left with literally no resources to support themselves. Others need encouragement on how to safeguard what they do have, and file the necessary paperwork to ensure spousal and child support. Many need to prepare a budget sheet for the first time. And as a separation continues, women who might not have been accustomed to managing money need to look out for their financial futures.

Does this sound like you? Well, even if you have the most cooperative and infinitely wealthy spouse, my guess is that you can learn a great deal from this chapter. Reading these pages, you'll discover money-saving tips to slash expenses. Proper financial planning can't be stressed enough. Your future peace of mind and quality of life depend upon it. Let me give you a scenario. We'll call our friend Barbara.

Recently separated from her well-off husband, Barbara continued to enjoy the lifestyle she'd been accustomed to in her marriage—country club memberships, weekly salon and manicure appointments, and shopping at exclusive stores, even for groceries. Barbara didn't think she had a financial care in the world because her husband promised to take care of everything, and she knew he certainly had the means to do just that.

But as time went by, Barbara's husband started resenting that she continued to entertain friends extravagantly and volunteer her efforts rather than work for payment. The couple's three children were grown, with one in college and two in high school. Barbara's husband gradually diminished the funds she was used to receiving. And indeed when the couple divorced, Barbara was assigned an earning capacity. Needless to say, Barbara was dumbfounded. Soon she was in debt, and for a while, she struggled—a lifestyle she was *not* accustomed to.

Financial Realities

This little story is not meant to alarm. I use it to illustrate that the financial situation you see yourself in today might not be the one you face in six months or several years. You must think about your future. Don't continue to let a man do this for you.

Of course, your financial future does not have to be bleaker than the one you previously enjoyed. This is sometimes so. But in many cases, women find that they can manage better without a husband in the picture. How can this be?

Simple. Some husbands have bad habits. They might gamble, spend frivolously, even eat you out of house and home.

Assuming that you aren't already in deep debt, and that you have an adequate amount of child and perhaps spousal support, it's conceivable that you won't feel as drastic a pinch as you might have expected. I found when my husband left that the groceries went farther, I could keep the thermostat where I wanted it, and the water bill even went down!

Where money is concerned we all have worries. Having been raised by Depression-era parents, I inherited their fears. But they taught me to spend wisely and live frugally, to research investments (even the simplest purchases), to control what I can, and to let go of the rest. That means having a little faith even where finances are concerned. You'll be okay, most likely, if you use common sense and caution. And as author Suze Orman often points out in talk show appearances, the way you handle money is closely tied to your self-esteem. The deeper your financial woes, the more you probably need to work on your belief system. You can overcome your fear and misuse of money. But first things first.

Safeguarding Assets

An important step is to safeguard assets you already have. Think your spouse won't raid bank accounts, sell off stock, or cash in insurance policies? Guess again. It's been done to unsuspecting wives who thought emotionally, not practically.

When I discovered upsetting realities in my own marriage, I sought legal advice. I was told to safeguard assets, moving accounts into my own name. I felt my trust had been broken, and it was only natural that I'd want some reassurance and more control over the finances.

Is this raiding? No. I can honestly say I did not pillage or plunder those accounts. In fact, they grew under my management and were safeguarded until equitable distribution.

Is it mean-spirited? Again, I don't think so.

As women have shared their separation stories with me, it's ironic. The same men who passively sit back enjoying their wife's financial prowess later claim that she was controlling with money. They can't have it both ways. And certainly if a husband uses funds illicitly, he shouldn't be surprised when his behavior hastens even more control of the finances. This ensures that assets aren't bled, paychecks drunk or gambled away, or funds used to furnish a mistress's apartment.

My advice to any woman facing separation is to safeguard assets, transferring liquid accounts into your name alone. If your husband begs forgiveness, he may understand your resolve to protect funds. He might willingly sign any documents to effect this. But some banks will require only one party of a joint account to close it out and open another.

On the day my husband walked out the door, we had only one joint bank account and credit card. The checking had a low balance, and that night I closed the credit card account. Unfortunately, that left me without a credit card, and I learned quickly that every woman, married or not, should have a VISA or MasterCard held in her own name. Still, going without a credit card for a few weeks was better than being responsible later for any joint debt racked up. And if your spouse is vindictive or addictive, believe me, you could be in for trouble if you don't close down any joint credit. So one last time—do not continue to share a credit line with your estranged husband.

Other assets such as life insurance policies, stocks, mutual funds, bonds, and other investments are usually more complex. Most will require both parties' signatures to liquidate. However, don't let too much time pass before you review these, and safeguard them as well. Your husband's new girlfriend just might show up at a brokerage firm trying to sign your name to release funds, or worse yet, you may have forgotten that power of attorney you signed years ago. Notify all financial institutions of your separation and require them to ask for identification before your signature is signed to anything.

For instance, to prevent a spouse from running off with the cash value of a life insurance policy, you might want to become the owner of that policy. Courts can sometimes mandate that your husband maintain a life insurance policy at least while you are separated. If you followed the guidelines of accumulating account numbers and balances outlined in Chapter 1, you should be in pretty good shape with a paper trail. Make copies of these statements for your attorney. The real tragedy occurs when a wife hasn't a clue what accounts they hold and what her husband's pension looks like. Remember, knowledge is power. Knowledge also means less anxiety.

One last caveat here on the subject of safeguarding. If you are tempted to dip into any marital monies during your separation, just remember that you will have to account for these funds at equitable distribution. This isn't play money. It's not even a loan. It's just money that you intend to protect until it can be divided equitably (not necessarily equally, mind you, but equitably). If support payments stop or fall behind and you need to protect a marital asset (such as your home) with this money to pay the mortgage, keep good records. And, of course, consult your attorney if you have one.

Filing for Support

Speaking of attorneys, many women have the misguided notion that you must have a lawyer to collect child support. This is partially untrue. I say partially because one of the first moves you should make in a separation is to file for child and spousal support. You do not need an attorney to do this.

It's paramount that you file as soon as possible because you will be assigned a conference date six to eight weeks away, when support will be decided. The longer you delay, the longer it will take. Also, the date of petition is the effective date, so it's best to do this quickly. File for support first and get a hearing date set. Then concentrate on finding an attorney (see Chapter 4).

To file for support, contact your family court division. Chances are good there will be a recorded message with instructions on filing for support. Or again, if you have already retained an attorney, follow that advice.

The paperwork that you need to fill out, including a budget sheet of living expenses and a statement of your income, deserves careful attention. Frequently this information will set the tone for all future support hearings and decisions. These sworn statements show the parties need for and/or ability to pay support. Thus, the sleuth work you did gathering documents, pay stubs, tax returns, and paid bill statements will assist you in accurately filling out the required forms.

Some women frequently forget the incidental expenses any family incurs. This is a big mistake. Those items you generally pay cash for include newspapers, school lunches, baby-sitters, preschool tuition, haircuts, gifts (including those for children's birthday parties and holidays), entertainment (such as movie admission, video rentals, or cable TV), household cleaning, and commuting or transportation costs (such as filling your gasoline tank or bus or subway fare to work). Your attorney, or perhaps the clerks present when you file for support, will give you a budget sheet with categories to jog your memory. Use this as a guideline, but brainstorm for any expense categories that are unique to your family. The parent who retains custody of the children always has higher incidental expenses.

Some states only consider the incomes of the parents when determining support awards. Others consider household income. Thus, if you or your estranged is cohabiting during your separation, this could influence your support figure.

Of course, it's wise to reach an agreement on your own, called a consent order, rather than rely upon the discretion of a hearing officer or judge. The family court system is one overloaded with cases and fraught with discord. Decisions rendered by third parties might be unfair, arbitrary, and difficult to overcome in the months and years ahead.

You know your situation better than anyone, and you have the better chance of getting the level of support that you and your children require if you can discuss things rationally. Armed with the appropriate income data for each of you, ask your attorney (or go to the public library) to look at the support guidelines that many states publish.

Unless your case is complex, or you simply cannot get the other side to negotiate, try to reach an agreement outside of a hearing. Besides, support hearings are rarely run on time. Every minute your attorney waits in the hallway racks up your bill, sometimes by hundreds of dollars before you even begin presenting your case.

Some final words regarding support. It can usually be modified at any time, but you may want to pay careful attention to the language in your court or consent order. Federal law required all support orders issued after January 1, 1994 to provide for wage attachment. It's more reliable, and today wage attachment is common.

Also, beware of the income tax ramifications. It's best to designate a certain portion for spousal support (temporary alimony, which is taxable income) and another for child support (nontaxable). If support is awarded without being broken down, you may be liable for tax on the entire amount. In addition, it might be wise to use the term "without prejudice" in your document. Without such wording, one of you would have to prove a change in circumstance before any future modification.

Being as specific as possible eliminates future hassles and legal fees. For instance, your support order will likely state that one of you is to maintain the family's health insurance and reimburse for out-of-pocket medical expenses (co-pay amounts and prescriptions). Be sure to set a time limit for reimbursement, such as within thirty days. This eliminates one party withholding payment as a control issue.

Tracking Down Deadbeat Dads

If either party fails to provide support as outlined in your order, the wronged spouse can present a motion for contempt of court. Your attorney will typically be the one to handle this, but anyone can present a motion before a judge. Alleged violators will have the opportunity to explain why they have not complied with the order, and why they shouldn't be held in contempt. If the hearing officer or judge does find the party in contempt, assets can be seized, fines levied, or jail sentences invoked. Don't let too much time pass before initiating contempt proceedings because it may take weeks beyond the initial motion for a hearing.

Of course, if the father has skipped town, it might seem more difficult to collect child support, but there are ways of locating him. Your state's child support agency can do a parent locator search. Thanks to computer technology, it's possible to track down a deadbeat dad who has moved across state lines. In compliance with federal law, employers must turn in the names, addresses, dates of birth, and social security numbers of all new hires on or after January 1, 1998. This was designed in part to nab deadbeat parents. Here are other measures:

- Many states also withhold from commissions, dividends, retirement benefits, and lottery winnings. Some revoke the professional or driver's licenses of deadbeat parents.
- In many states, motor vehicle registration records are open to the public. Call the bureau with your husband's name, social security number, and date of birth to find out what vehicles are listed under his name, as well as his current address.
- Visit your county's taxation department or deeds and property assessment office; these are all open to the public. If you have no luck, request that your county clerk of courts do a property search.

- Allow the Internal Revenue Service (IRS) to intercept a delinquent payer's income tax refund. Your child support agency verifies the amount overdue and submits the case to the IRS.
- Ask your agency's caseworker to obtain information from your estranged spouse's bank, mortgage company, or other financial institutions to determine his holdings. It's possible to put liens on real estate or personal property and to attach bank accounts to collect past-due support.

You can tackle all of these suggestions on your own and with no cost other than your time. Advocacy and support organizations might offer additional ideas. One such agency is the Association for Children for Enforcement of Support (ACES), based in Toledo, Ohio (1-800-537-7072). Keep on top of your case, and if these measures fail, you can always hire a private attorney to investigate matters. However, this would be the most expensive route to go.

Credit—Establishing It and Getting Rid of It

As I've already stated, every woman should have a major credit card in her name alone. A credit card is important for many reasons. For starters, it helps you establish a good credit profile. It's handy in an emergency, and eliminates the need to carry cash. It makes ordering by telephone or the Internet or securing an airline reservation or hotel room a snap. Finally, it gives additional protection with life insurance (if, heaven forbid, you are in an airline accident and booked with that card), and it allows you to put an item in dispute if there is a problem with the merchandise.

However, while credit cards might lubricate the economy, they wreak havoc on people's budgets. So here I'll discuss how to establish and maintain good credit health, which is preferable to dodging creditors, declaring bankruptcy, or having a bad credit history haunt you. Bad credit is not only hazardous to your financial future but to your career. The Fair Credit Reporting Act permits employers to access your credit record, and some companies view the report as a sign of your fiscal responsibility.

For starters, if you cancelled any joint credit cards with your husband, as I've already suggested, then you may be left without a card. Check with the bank where your checking and other accounts are held. Often, you're entitled to a major credit card, so all you need to do is fill out the application. Be certain when listing your income that you include spousal support in addition to your own earned income. This will help process the application without question or delay.

Depending upon your income (or lack of it), you might be turned down for a credit card. If that's the case, you can begin to build a credit history by obtaining a secured card, where you transfer money out of savings into a separate account that the credit card then draws from. Essentially, you can't spend money you don't already have.

Of course, it's great if you can get paid someway to use a card, as in frequent flier points, rebates, or car discounts. But if you have to pay an outrageous annual fee, forget it. Budget-minded consumers shouldn't pay anything over $50 for the convenience of credit because there are cards with no annual fees available. Therefore, the perk has to be pretty good to even consider paying any fee.

Establishing credit might be a whole lot tougher if you are trying to clean up a poor credit history. You might want to contact one of the three credit-reporting services to see what your history looks like. I'll discuss this in detail in the coming pages. You'd be surprised to find that charge cards you rarely use or thought you cancelled might still show up as available credit. This could work against you if a potential lender feels you have too much access to credit. When determining whether to loan you money, creditors use a process called credit scoring. They even look at the number of recent inquiries into your credit record. So write to any companies whose cards you no longer use. Ask them to cancel the account and report that to the credit services.

While it may seem daunting, you do have several paths out of deep debt. If you're really in trouble, seek help from Consumer Credit Counseling (1-800-388-2227) or the National Foundation for Consumer Credit (1-800-284-1723). Both are nonprofit organizations with centers nationwide. Some are free or charge less than $25 to consolidate your debt and deal with creditors. Beware of fraudulent telemarketers who promise to clean up credit reports for a fee. Third-party collectors often don't have the ability to remove damaging information previously reported by a bank.

Debtors Anonymous might not work with those you owe, but the meetings and support will help you rely less on credit and make sound financial choices.

Filing for bankruptcy, in which you ask a federal judge to repay creditors on different terms (often cents on the dollar), should be your absolute last resort. Such a move stays on your credit report for ten years, and future creditors will shun you for car loans, mortgages, and credit lines. Be prepared that a vindictive spouse may threaten to take this route. If you have joint assets, however, these usually can't be touched, at least by the creditors. They'll go after anything that exists solely in your husband's name. Also, overdue taxes, alimony, and child support are not discharged through bankruptcy.

Some other avenues you can take to clear credit card debt include:

- Call creditors on your own to work out a repayment schedule. This shows that you're taking responsibility. Individual creditors are usually willing to work with you; they know they stand a better chance of collecting more money this way than if you proceed with a bankruptcy filing.
- Ask the creditor for a letter of agreement that holds you responsible for half of the debt. Bear in mind, you may not get anywhere with this request. However, if you explain that you are divorcing and can't pay the entire debt, the company might listen. Offer that if they'll send you this agreement in writing, you'll find the money to pay off your half.
- Paying off the highest interest rates first. For instance, pay off a balance that's growing at 20 percent before working on the 11-percent problem.

- Transfer balances to other low-interest charge cards while you use other strategies in this list to pay off debt.
- Revamp your budget by trimming expenses and raising extra cash.
- Tap savings accounts, money market funds, or stocks. (If jointly held these are considered marital property and you had better consult your attorney). If an income-earning account is yours alone, you are better off using that cash in getting rid of debt that costs you an additional 18 to 20 percent each month.
- Consolidate debt under a home-equity loan. (This would require cooperation from your estranged spouse if you jointly hold the mortgage).
- Borrow from family if all other options aren't possible.

The best investment you can make if you are in credit card debt is to pay off these balances and then charge only what you can pay in full each month. Life is 18 to 20 percent more expensive for those who carry credit card balances, and you don't need the additional anxiety.

If you have marital debt that technically you are both liable for, you need to be very careful with any promises your husband might make to handle that debt. Even if it is ultimately written in a divorce settlement that he will pay the debt, you might still be held liable from the bank's point of view. To protect your credit, ask for the amount in the settlement and make sure you retire the debt before you spend the money on anything else.

Throw away any new credit card solicitations you receive. I don't recommend cutting up all your credit cards; having at least one major credit card can be handy. However, if temptation and impulsive use of cards is a problem, try freezing them. That's right. Freeze your credit cards in a small bowl of water. By the time they thaw, you may have rethought the need for a purchase and decided you can live without it.

Obtaining a Credit Report

It's to your advantage to determine what credit reporting services think about you. This way, you can correct any errors before you apply for important credit, such as a mortgage or car loan (sometimes applied for on short notice). In most states, the fee for this report is $8; however, if you've been denied credit, employment, insurance, or housing, you are entitled to a free copy of your credit report within sixty days of the denial. Here are the major reporting services:

Equifax 1-800-685-1111 www.equifax.com
P.O. Box 105873
Atlanta, GA 30348

Experian 1-800-682-7654 www.experian.com
P.O. Box 2104
Allen, TX 75013

Trans Union Corp. 1-800-916-8800 www.transunion.com
P.O. Box 390
Springfield, PA 19064

Raising Quick Cash

Many separated women find they need to raise extra cash because their spouse left them in a financial lurch. Others want to move on with their lives, perhaps physically moving households. Still others want to build a financial cushion.

In fact, if for no other reason than to boost your savings, reading the following tips could help build that emergency fund everyone should have. Financial planners encourage people to stash away six to eight months of living expenses in a money market fund. If you lose your job, or if your estranged spouse loses his and falls behind in support payments, you have money to fall back upon. Peruse the following list to raise quick cash:

- Hold a yard or garage sale. Refrain from selling treasured heirlooms, antiques, or personal belongings that your estranged spouse may claim later. Concentrate on items that have little significant or sentimental value, or those belonging to you or your children. If you don't want the bother of a sale, take the items to an auction house or flea market dealer.
- Remember the line in Disney's *Toy Story* where one toy, fearing replacement, says, "We're next month's garage sale fodder for sure." Toys and no-longer-needed baby items are sure bets for clearing clutter and raising cash. List popular items in your local advertising supplement where anyone can place a free ad for things $25 or less. It doesn't sound like major cash, but if you consider all the baby items you may have in the attic or basement, old bikes, outdated software, games, or videotapes,

you'd be surprised how quickly you amass a few hundred dollars.

- Return never-worn clothing or unwrapped items to stores for full credit, a cash refund, or an even exchange. Of course, this means clothing with the tags on, appliances and toys never used, books never read, or compact discs never taken out of the shrink-wrap. Again, you'd be surprised how much money is returned to you. If no cash equivalent is available, take a store credit to purchase items you or your children do need. It's like going on a shopping spree without spending any money. Or, take the credit and shop ahead for birthday or holiday gifts.
- Ask for refunds for products that didn't live up to the manufacturer's promise, or services poorly rendered. No one likes a constant complainer, but if you don't speak up, you don't allow others to produce a better product or service. So if a restaurant meal isn't satisfactory, call the manager. If an item has a money-back guarantee, save the package details. In past years, I've been refunded money from lawn-care products, diaper and pharmaceutical companies, and restaurants. My online service provider granted me additional hours because of problems with the service.
- Refinance your existing mortgage if you can obtain a new mortgage at least one percentage point below your existing rate. Of course, if the mortgage is jointly held, this might not be possible until a divorce is final.
- File amended tax returns if you forgot a legitimate deduction that could have saved you money or

enhanced a refund. If you were accustomed to filing joint returns, this might require cooperation. But if you filed separately, it's a fairly painless and completely legal way of seeing some cash. You don't need to hire an accountant, either. TurboTax, MacInTax, or Kiplinger's Tax Cut software make amending returns and preparing new ones pretty simple.

- Change your withholding at work. If you traditionally receive a large income-tax refund, this could be a sign you're paying too much in withholdings. So fill out the appropriate papers to effect the change.
- Work overtime periodically, ask for a raise, or boost your rates if you're self-employed. These strategies impact your career, but often people procrastinate in seeking solutions with their current job. More income could be around the corner.
- Moonlight. As I said promoting my book *Writing For Money,* writing is the one form of moonlighting the boss is least likely to complain about. Thus, I'm a firm believer in moonlighting for many reasons.

For starters, moonlighting simply has a different cache about it. But you must choose your options carefully. If you told your boss that you were planning to work from 6 to 10 PM at the local Kmart, she might not be too thrilled, and in fact, may feel a bit threatened that you're giving your all to another employer.

But tell that same boss that you're going home to put the finishing touches on an article for publication, and she might surprise you with, "Oh, isn't that nice. When will it appear? How did you come to write for that magazine?" You get the picture. Moonlighting gives many a chance to turn a hobby into profit, and since we generally enjoy our hobbies, we tend to be happier doing the work. Therein lies another advantage.

Certainly as author of another book, *Working at Home While the Kids Are There, Too,* I have ideas for you to consider in your brainstorming process:

Administrative assistance, for if you know how to type or maintain a database, you could find your services in demand by churches, small businesses, or entrepreneurs who cannot afford full-time personnel. You could advertise your services to jobseekers who need resumes and cover letters as well.

Arts and crafts, including writing as well as making pottery, baskets, holiday crafts, gift packages, and more.

Computer consulting, if you know the technical aspects, allows you to teach others how to operate their systems and software. You might design web sites for small businesses, individuals, or organizations that do not have large enough budgets to employ a firm.

Tax preparation is a seasonal way of making additional income if you're qualified to do the work.

Tutoring allows you to put that undergraduate degree or the skills you've acquired to work, helping others at the same time. You might even pick up extra money by teaching a noncredit class through a continuing education program near you, meeting new adult friends at the same time.

- Ask for financial aid if you're a student. Ask the college's financial aid office for assistance or turn to your reference librarian for resources like *The College Costs and Financial Aid Handbook* (published by the College

Board) or the books published by Peterson's including *Financing Graduate School.* In addition, the U.S. Dept. of Education has free pamphlets and materials by calling 1-800-433-3243. Ask about Pell grants (scholarships that aren't to be repaid), Perkins loans, and Stafford loans (both with low-interest rates).

Living on a Budget

Whether you dig out of debt, save for your own legal defense fund, or spend less to invest more, learning to live on a budget is helpful. Some families put this in written form and live by the numbers each month.

While I've never committed my plan to paper, I do believe budgets are great, even in your head. For me, living on less is a challenge and even can be fun.

First, figure out where your money is going. Write down each expense as you pay for it. Keep a notebook handy or create a worksheet on your computer. Software programs such as Quicken can help you track your expenditures and balance your checkbook each month, too.

Cut out unnecessary expenses and resist impulse purchases. Often, you don't need these items. If you add up incidentals like coffee, snacks, and lunches out, you could save hundreds of dollars each year.

Direct depositing your paycheck means you're less likely to ask for cash back that you spend indiscriminately. Avoid overdrafts or have overdraft protection (though balancing your account and using self-discipline is best). Watch ATM fees by withdrawing from machines in the system to avoid surcharges. Never opt for deferred billing.

Use only one major credit card which should have a thirty-day grace period between the end of the billing cycle and the payment due date. Don't take out cash advances or use those convenience checks they provide. Treated the same as cash advances, they're one of the most expensive ways of borrowing money (without the protection/dispute resolution credit cards carry).

Drive a used (perhaps gently used) automobile. You can read more about car purchases and care in Chapter 8. And never—absolutely never—shop when you're hungry!

Accepting Help When You Need It

Many women who go through a separation feel uneasy about accepting help from family, friends, or organizations. Often, they feel as if they need so much—from emotional support and caring for the children to legal and financial help—they are too proud to ask for assistance when it's warranted. Swallow your pride temporarily and do ask for the support that could make your life and your children's lives that much better.

I understand what it's like. When my husband left, I certainly faced a loss of household income, yet I still had two children with some special needs. It seemed everything had to be haggled over by attorneys who billed at $150 an hour. Fortunately, help stepped forward. My first attorney often deducted items from the bill whenever she could. Friends pitched in to watch my boys whenever possible, and they never charged a cent. My oldest son's school gave us free turkeys at Thanksgiving. The preschool director assured me that scholarship funds were available since the developmental delays of my youngest made preschool paramount.

Sure it felt uncomfortable. Where preschool was concerned, I had to live with a small amount of humiliation; the preschool program was featured in local newspapers. My mother-in-law was written about as founder of the program—a program that now supported her grandson, so of course I felt angry. But I got over it, and I realized that someday I'd be able to help someone else in need. Other women I interviewed accepted scholarships, received food pantry supplies, and did whatever else they could when their husbands bailed. We women are resourceful, but sometimes we do need to take people up on their offers to assist us. After all, it's only temporary.

Pinching Pennies

Have you ever noticed that certain well-off friends seem to be the best budget-minded souls around? That's no accident. You don't get wealthy by wasting money.

Similarly, you don't eliminate money worries or boost your savings by spending frivolously. For now, conserve your funds—whether you have to, or merely choose to. Let's begin our quest for eliminating unnecessary expenses.

Around the House

- Obtain a free energy audit from utility companies. An energy auditor will reveal places in your home where you could make improvements, conserve energy, and save money. For instance, you could insulate the outside of your hot water heater, turn the water temperature down, and set the thermostat back when you aren't home.

- Limit water usage by taking shorter showers or filling the bathtub halfway. Use mostly cold water for laundry. Refrain from watering the lawn, or avoid this when the moisture will evaporate quickly. Install low-flow devices on showerheads and faucets.
- Use open windows instead of air conditioning unless it's absolutely unbearable. Landscaping shaded areas around your home may also reduce air conditioning costs.
- Purchase your phones rather than lease them. Eliminate optional services on your bill that you don't need. Make long-distance calls at off hours or send e-mail instead. Dial direct. Look up phone numbers yourself.

TRAVELING

- Pump your own gas and get to know where the lowest-price gas stations are in your community. Keep your engine tuned and your tires inflated to the proper pressure.
- Shop around for the best rental car rates. Check with your auto insurance agent before paying extra for rental insurance. Your existing policy may already cover you.
- Book airline reservations in advance or at the last minute using reduced-price Internet fares. A Saturday night stay usually reduces costs.

- Look for nonstop flights if your children must travel unaccompanied to visit their father. Some airlines have doubled surcharges for unaccompanied kids.
- If you belong to a motor club, ask for discounts. Give your frequent flier mileage number for flights, rental cars, and hotel rooms.

EATING AND ENTERTAINING

- Avoid convenience stores. Warehouse clubs and low-priced food markets often reduce your grocery bill.
- Clip coupons and combine them with on-sale items. I trimmed a grocery receipt from $51.46 to $13.97 using my frequent customer card, manufacturer's coupons, and a $10 gift certificate. If you don't have a substantial coupon, buy generic store brands.
- Purchase items on sale, including some produce and meats, and freeze them for later use. The same goes for cheese, tortillas, coffee, and refrigerated cookie dough. Sometimes, buying a small stand-alone freezer pays for itself in convenience and the savings from on-sale items.
- Find creative uses for things. Stale (but not moldy) bread can be frozen to make French toast or bread crumbs. Freeze unused milk if you'll be traveling, and use it to make milk shakes when you get home. A surplus of Halloween candy can go into the freezer and be doled out for school lunches.
- Invite friends for potluck dinners or pizza made from scratch. Have relatives over for breakfast or simple lunches instead of fancy dinners. Or cut main courses and opt for dessert and coffee.

STAYING HEALTHY

- Take care of your health with preventative care, including dental cleanings and routine exams. If ill, go to the doctor before you get sicker.
- When at the doctor, ask for prescription drug samples. Explain that your health plan doesn't include prescription coverage (or has a high co-pay). Often physicians have a stash in a supply cabinet.
- When getting a prescription, ask for the generic alternative if it's available. Ask for your doctor to write this on the actual prescription.
- Know where the discount pharmacies are, and call to compare drug prices. Consider mail-order or online pharmacies.
- Use coupons for over-the-counter medications or vitamins, or buy generic store brands, comparing the ingredients and also watching for sales. Seek a refund if there is a guarantee on a product that didn't work well. Some prescribed medicines even have rebates. Or, stores with a pharmacy offer gift certificates if you fill your prescription with them. Thus, you might be $25 richer merely choosing their pharmacy.
- Go to free health screenings, and sign up for low-cost or no-cost health insurance (usually for kids) if eligible.

OUTFITTING THE KIDS AND YOURSELF

- Buy clothes at end-of-season sales. This works for Christmas sweaters to swimsuits and beach towels. At a January clearance, I snagged a casual coat that was missing two buttons for under $10. Turns out, extra buttons came inside the coat to sew on.

- Keep an eye out at yard and garage sales for kids' play clothes and dress-up treasures.
- Choose next year's Halloween costumes at more than half off the day after Halloween. But don't wait too long because merchandise like this goes fast.
- If you have siblings of the same sex, make use of hand-me-down items. They are new to younger siblings, especially if they weren't even born yet to see them worn!
- Shop at stores where merchandise is guaranteed or discounts given. Sears Kidvantage program earns you discounts. And with boys, when the knees on jeans invariably rub through, the pants are automatically replaced in the same size.
- Swap clothing with relatives or friends who have children the genders of your own. If asked for gift suggestions from grandparents or anyone else, mention clothing the kids might need.
- Browse the racks of second-hand clothing stores or visit yard sales in exclusive neighborhoods. You'll find many selections for yourself, including suits for work or evening wear—even accessories at much more affordable prices. Kids clothing will often be the better brand names.

Trimming Holiday Expenses

Your Christmas tree isn't the only item needing trimming when you're separated. Chances are you can free up some extra money by making the holidays more affordable. And if conserving finances isn't a good enough reason, think of your sanity. Since you've already got enough stress, here are ways to simplify the holidays:

- Shop sales throughout the year. I found Dilbert magnets, pens, and pencils on clearance in office and bookstores. One year, I stocked up on wooden train tracks and accessories. These virtually never go on sale, but with a store's liquidation, I saved 30 percent plus an additional 10 percent with a frequent-purchase card.
- Stash away small or token gifts by shopping early. Sometimes your employer or clients offer freebies. Save some of these to include in holiday giving.
- Take advantage of after-holiday sales. Why anyone would purchase Christmas lights, garland, artificial trees, cards, and wrapping paper at full price is beyond me. All of these items are at least 50 percent off the day after Christmas. Throughout January, prices are slashed even further.
- Make homemade gifts for some relatives, friends, and teachers. Something as simple as homemade bread or cookies can be wrapped with festive ribbon tied around cellophane.
- Stock up on baking supplies during the holidays when stores run sales. Watch your Sunday newspaper supplements for coupons too. With a sale and coupon combination, you'll have cookie and cake decorating supplies for other occasions throughout the year.

- Create a grab-bag with extended family to cut down on the number of gifts. Ship presents early so that you can mail packages at the lowest rates.
- Send virtual greeting cards to those with online access. Or, use postcards and let your children create a family Web page that serves as your holiday newsletter. Send thank-you messages the same way.
- Entertain simply with potluck dinners or merely coffee and dessert get-togethers.
- Suggest items that you or your children need to those who ask for ideas. Often, relatives and friends want to help by providing toys or clothing that might strain your budget.
- Settle on one large gift if your children are old enough to understand. For instance, if your kids could use a computer for schoolwork, such a purchase makes sense (and might qualify as a partial tax write-off if you're self-employed or moonlight from home).
- Combine giving, especially if you and your estranged spouse have an amicable relationship. No sense both of you buying holidays gifts for your children. Put both names on one set of gifts.
- Donate with a little creativity. If you're conserving cash, you can still be generous with gifts of your time or gently used toys or outgrown clothing to food pantries and social service agencies.

Managing Your Financial Future

A marital separation often places women at a financial crossroad. Even if you master nothing else but your finances, I can assure you that you'll step into the future with a lot more confidence and security.

So what about that future? It's there, although at this juncture merely getting through today and tomorrow seems a challenge. The wise woman plans for her financial future and avoids the mistake of making emotional decisions versus practical ones.

BEATING A LACK OF SELF-CONFIDENCE

Some women procrastinate, executing poor financial decisions because of their own lack of self-confidence where money is concerned. Particularly if they had husbands who were the primary breadwinners, managed their investments, and paid the bills, the thought of instantly moving into these roles is daunting.

Women who work in jobs that don't carry clout may also lack self-confidence. Mind you, I believe the day-care provider is just as capable of managing her assets as the vice president of a corporation. Unfortunately, as women we sometimes talk ourselves into a diminished role. Our self-esteem suffers in more than our career.

If this sounds like you, here's an encouraging thought. Financial writer Linda Stern wrote in *Family Money* that "women can double a dollar faster than any old-fashioned broker can say, 'I love bull markets.'" I wholeheartedly believe this. And hopefully, so will you.

College Concerns and Retirement Nest Eggs

As mothers we are all concerned that our children obtain a college education, especially if we had that privilege. Few of us, however, can get the cooperation of our spouses (sometimes the same ones we helped put through school!) to ensure this for our sons and daughters. As I write this book, my own state of Pennsylvania does not mandate that fathers help with higher education, even if they can afford to do so. It's painful to see your estranged run off, frivolously spending your children's college funds. However, financial planners can't emphasize enough the importance of securing your own retirement before financing a child's education.

"I can't do that," you might say, feeling as I did that the mere thought was selfish. But it's true. Your children can obtain loans and grants. They can also complete their degrees in intervals, over a period of years. No one else besides you will secure your retirement. And since many women lack pensions and live longer than men, don't think you're set if you only remarry.

Don't beat yourself up about boosting your own savings. Actually, it's better if assets are not accumulated in your children's names. When they apply for financial aid, they stand a better chance of obtaining it if they are poor and you have the money. Also, under the Uniform Gift to Minors Act, any money left to your children is theirs. They can spend it on college tuition or a sports car. This is another reason to seriously consider asset allocation.

Using a Financial Planner

Years ago when I was practically a newlywed, one of the best decisions I made was to sit down with a financial planner to analyze my finances. Believe me, there wasn't much to analyze, and I'm certainly not making Danielle Steel royalties now! But the mere act meant I committed the time to studying where I was, setting goals for where I wanted to be, and figuring out what was important financially. It also established a pattern of regular saving and dollar-cost averaging (more on this later). The planner who helped me came from a trusted personal referral, and while he did not charge a fee for advice given, he was making a commission on the mutual funds or insurance policies my husband and I invested in. Financial planners are compensated this way, or else they charge for their counsel. Years later, I recognized the appeal of no-load funds, and I transferred money into new accounts that I managed on my own through reading and investment education, but I learned early to set aside money. That lesson endures over time.

In the initial stages of separation, you probably aren't thinking of using a financial planner. You have an attorney giving you most of your advice. However, as you travel the litigation path and get closer to a financial settlement, you should analyze your finances, perhaps with professional help. Your attorney is trained to interpret laws, not tax regulations or long-term financial plans.

BECOMING A SAVVY INVESTOR

From the start, let's make one thing clear. Handling money isn't like brain surgery. No one will die, even if you make a few errors along the way.

Surprisingly, there are a number of truly simple steps you can take to increase your financial prowess. Reading is paramount. Read the business page. Peruse *The Wall Street Journal* at work or in the library. Read magazines devoted to personal finances, particularly for strategic end-of-year money moves. Don't just toss the prospectus you receive into the recycling bin.

By reading literature regarding the mutual funds or stocks you've invested in, you get a clear picture of how your funds are performing. For instance, if you own multiple mutual funds, review the stock picks chosen for you. It's possible you're duplicating your efforts and might be paying unnecessary management fees. Consolidate your accounts, if that's the case.

In addition, it's wise to expand your understanding of personal finance. Attend financial seminars and bookstore discussions featuring financial authors. You might even try watching the financial channels. Rather than football, there's the annual "Money Bowl" on CNBC each New Year's Day.

Web surfers can take advantage of the Internet to learn about mutual funds and stock performance. Most investment companies provide a wealth of information to aid your decision making. Just do a search with any of the major search engines, like Yahoo.com or AltaVista.com. Quicken is a leading manufacturer of personal finance and small business software, and they have a Web site filled with tools and information. If you're in the market for better buys on insurance, mortgage rates, or credit cards, the Internet can help you as well. Here are a few more tips:

- Call the Certified Financial Planner Board of Standards for the free booklet, "What You Should Know about Financial Planning." Reach them at 1-888-237-6275.
- In "Social Security: What Every Woman Should Know," you'll read that if your marriage lasted ten years

or more, you may be eligible to receive benefits on your ex-husband's record. Visit a Social Security office near you and ask for this information, free of charge.

- Write for the Energy Savers booklet, c/o Post Office Box 3048, Dept. P, Merrifield, VA 22116, or call 1-800-363-3732. It's got money-saving tips, too.

Many continuing education departments have noncredit courses that teach you how to read the stock pages, understand bonds, or build a balanced portfolio. Each woman's situation is different, depending upon her age, earning capacity, goals, and needs, so it's nearly impossible to give blanket advice.

Having said that, however, there are a few tried and true investment strategies. For starters, set up an IRA, SEP-IRA, or Keogh if you're self-employed (or a 401(k) through your employer) and contribute to it at regular intervals. For instance, had you invested regularly throughout the worst decade of the twentieth century (1928-1938), you still could have averaged 7 percent per year in returns despite the Great Depression. That's the beauty of dollar-cost averaging—investing evenly over time for long-term gain.

In addition, reinvest all dividends and treat bonuses or found money as just that. Don't rush right out to spend a windfall. Sock it away into savings. Over time, the stock market has been the highest performing investment vehicle most people have. Of course, there is risk, but the object is to buy and hold. Do this when you are young and by retirement, you'll be in for quite a nice surprise.

Finally, focus on no-load mutual funds or direct purchase stock plans. Charles Carlson has written *No-Load Stocks.* As he explains, a surprising number of companies offer stock to individual investors in what are known as direct investment plans (DIPs) and dividend reinvestment plans (DRIPs). Investors might only purchase a few shares, certainly a lot fewer than a round lot of one hundred shares that most brokers would require. Their money continues to compound thanks to dividends, stock splits, and very low investment expenses. As soon as you accumulate one hundred shares of a company stock, it's wise to request the actual stock certificates. This way, you can sell quickly if you need to by going to a brokerage firm (discount and Internet brokers would charge less than full-service firms).

An Important Rule for the Road

Before you set out on your investment journey, remember an important caveat. Make no quick financial moves for at least six months after your separation, especially those that lock you into an investment or carry a high amount of risk. Give yourself time to ponder your choices, educate yourself, and make wise moves. And, check out the resources in this book's appendix.

If Remarriage Is on the Horizon

If a wayward spouse has jeopardized your financial position, think carefully before co-mingling finances again. I am not suggesting that you never remarry or take out a mortgage with a new husband. Prenuptial agreements are discussed in detail in Chapter 4. You should definitely look back at that section if you are planning to remarry.

Chapter Seven

Carving Out a Career

What's a woman to do when she's been predominantly a helpmate, mother, and homemaker for at least the past several years of her marriage, and suddenly she's faced with the added responsibility of becoming primary breadwinner?

During a separation, some women answer this question with a sense of panic. This chapter will help you carve out a career path that's right for you, and move ahead in the work you currently pursue. It will deal with the necessary steps to finding work—creating resumés and cover letters, identifying companies and getting to decision makers, interviewing and following up as well as career-boosting strategies.

When my own separation began, I had a career, but it sure was curtailed. When my son Alex was born two years prior, I had put everything on the back burner until my premature son's health improved. Finding myself alone was not what I had anticipated. I did panic a little, wondering if I'd be able to build my home-based writing business back and get the work accomplished while continuing to meet my children's needs. Or, should I opt right away for a full-time job? Of course, I felt pressured by my estranged husband. Suddenly the writing I did, which once brought him pride and a few nice perks, became "that hobby" I worked at.

But through it all, I held my head high. I always look at the classified ads (though as we'll learn this isn't the best avenue for job searches). I went on several interviews, and mailed dozens more resumés and letters. In one instance, where I knew full well I was qualified for a special events position, I helped a good friend of mine write a resumé for the same company. Turns out she got a job, and someone else was hired for the spot I coveted. But I did the right thing in helping her, and I'm convinced it was an indication I was still needed on the homefront.

In those initial weeks, another wise advisor put it bluntly. "The object here isn't to run to the nearest McDonald's and get hired. Give yourself time to find what's best for you." How very true! Time does have a way of lighting our paths, even professionally. As long as you explore all your options, you'll do just fine.

Starting from Scratch

Though that sense of panic is indeed very real for some women, I hope this chapter will help put your mind at ease. Even if you lack much formal education and have confined yourself to homemaking or volunteer work in recent years, you do have skills that will translate into the workplace. Career counselors call these "transferable skills." Furthermore, you have more options than women faced twenty or thirty years ago.

Become a trend spotter as best you can when you begin a career makeover. This gives you a feel for what occupations are hot and which aren't hiring as well. Should you need to take additional courses or obtain another degree, you'll make wiser decisions. Read books, peruse the daily paper, and collect magazine articles. Some publications that I've found particularly helpful in spotting trends include *USA Today* and *The Wall Street Journal* as well as *Futurist* or *American Demographics,* which keep a pulse on consumer trends (these are also a bit pricey, so you might want to check out your local library's periodical holdings). Continue to spot trends by listening to talk radio, televised interviews, and newscasts.

Of course, if you work in a particular industry, there might be trade journals to keep your eyes on. Use *The Gale Directory of Publications,* available at your local library, to help you find these professional periodicals. While there, check out *Standard & Poor's Register of Corporations, Directors and Executives* as well as the *Encyclopedia of Associations* to find groups with membership rosters that might be useful. Your reference librarian might also have a copy of the *Occupational Outlook Handbook,* published by the U.S. Department of Labor, Bureau of Labor Statistics. This handy resource gives you an overview of jobs needed now and into the future.

That takes care of the marketplace, but now let's turn our attention to you. Thirty years ago, Richard Nelson Bolles brought us one of the best-selling job search books ever with *What Color Is Your Parachute?* It's a quirky title for sure, but it demystifies the job-hunting process. The author guides you in learning to look for signs of achievement in yourself. You consider profound questions like what type of work makes you happy and what you feel you have to offer.

Take a legal pad and list all your skills. Really think here. Have you paid the family bills for years and researched purchases (including home computers and software)? Have you juggled the schedules of everyone in your household? What about volunteer work at church or the PTA? Have you held positions of authority on church or civic boards? Have you ever volunteered for a political campaign? Are you comfortable getting up in front of groups, teaching, or soliciting a cause?

This gives you something to fuel your brainstorming. Translated onto paper are things like organizational, research and budgetary skills; multi-tasking; effective time management; and leadership responsibilities. In addition, you might have excellent promotion and sales skills—and perhaps creative talents—if you've produced newsletters, reports, or flyers.

The shelves of your local bookstore or library probably have dozens of resources to help you discover actual job titles, salary potential, and qualifications. Some of these are listed in this chapter. But if you're looking for a handy workbook to help you identify your skill set and talents, turn the pages of *101 Ways To Power Up Your Job Search.*

Going for a Graduate Degree

Now might be the time to contemplate graduate school. Yes, you already have your hands full, but furthering your education may provide not only additional earning potential in the years to come, but a new focus that will force you out of the house and into the company of new friends and business contacts. It may also give a much-needed confidence boost where your skills are concerned, and broaden your career options.

Even if you begin only on a part-time basis, it may be wise to take the required standardized tests (GRE, LSAT, etc.) and do a little research. Peterson's publishes a wide range of guides that you can discover in the bookstore or at www.petersons.com. If financing graduate studies is a concern, be sure to check out *Financing Graduate School* by Patricia McWade.

Self-knowledge Boosts Self-confidence

The best way to shelve that panic of re-entering the workforce is to get yourself out and mingling with other adults. Start putting yourself in settings where professionals get together. In many communities, there are a variety of networking and business groups comprised of women. Some of these meet for breakfast or lunch, sometimes at restaurants or even the book superstores. Most of the time, you can join these meetings on an informal basis on a few occasions before you might be required to become a dues-paying member (if there is a fee at all).

Call your local Chamber of Commerce for luncheon dates and after-hours gatherings. Investigate professional organizations that apply to your career. In my field of public relations and communications, groups like Public Relations Society of America (PRSA) and International Association of Business Communicators (IABC) have local chapters. If you can't find listings for their meetings in the business pages of your newspaper, call the department chairperson at a nearby university. Many national organizations maintain Web sites with this information.

Career placement offices are helpful, and so are the "adult re-entry" or "women's centers" at community colleges. Here, you'll find information and counseling, perhaps even testing, to help you objectively determine a proper career path.

Search Methods

What do most people do when they are in the market for a job or career advancement? They browse the newspaper classified ads or mail a massive stack of resumés to potential employers. Unfortunately, only a small percentage of these efforts succeed. Of course, it only takes one great interview and subsequent offer to make a career move, and classified ads shouldn't be ignored entirely. Still, you need to broaden your job-hunting horizons.

Reading Bolles' book, *What Color Is Your Parachute?,* you learn the practical lessons of job searching. You gain strength and confidence that you aren't the only one trying to uncover the hidden job market. Thus, when you begin your search, knocking on people's doors, sending letters, or following up correspondence with a phone call, you'll realize that we've all been along this journey at one point or another.

Depending upon your city, there might be books or directories pertaining to your region. Ask the reference librarian or do a search on the Internet. For instance, Benjamin Scott Publishing produces a series of job source books with contact names, addresses, and city information. Adams Media has a similar Job Bank Series of books dealing with major metropolitan cities.

Professionally published directories are great, but you can effect your own handy binder of information. As I've indicated, I took my time to learn about the job market, potential employers, and the qualifications they seek. Scanning the classifieds and spotting interesting articles in the business section, I often clip material out and immediately date it.

The next step is to paste or catalog this information in a binder sectioned off however you choose. Your organizational system could be alphabetical or categorized by industry. It could contain years worth of classified ads and background material.

Having such a resource compiled over time helps you identify hiring patterns and qualifications. If you aren't currently ready to make a career move, you can hang on to this information. In some cases, you'll get a feel for courses you might need to take or skills you need to update. When you do decide to search, you'll have a company, perhaps even a name and a phone number, from which to begin. Call to update your information. Contacts move on to other jobs and companies merge or relocate. Still, you'll find this is not only a tool in your search, but it aids in the important step of obtaining informational interviews, meetings with decision makers for the express purpose of picking their brains, gathering contacts, and learning about different companies. In addition, ask your alumni office at the college or university you attended for a printout of graduates working in your field. Approach them as an alum-made-good, asking them to share some insights on their success.

Use *The Job Bank Guide To Employment Services* published by Adams Media to find search firms and employment agencies that might also help your job search. Typically, search firms handle higher-level positions than employment agencies, where you might be required to pay a fee yourself for the matching service. But before we get too far along in the search process, let's focus on your qualifications.

Writing Your Resumé and Cover Letters

With plenty of excellent books to guide you and show examples of successful resumés in your chosen field, I'm certainly not going to duplicate that advice here. Use this section then to gather the data you'll need for your resumé, whether you do it yourself or rely upon the expertise of a professional writer or career counselor.

Using that legal pad you've already compiled some information on, now list achievements such as dollar figures produced, funds raised, or percentages of sales and productivity you increased. Write down the job responsibilities or projects you initiated and completed. Employers like to see signs of self-motivation and accomplishment. If you self-financed your education, note this also. Don't forget military background, educational credentials, outside interests, and special honors or achievements, even in professional or volunteer organizations. (One caution: If you list too many pro bono activities a potential employer might wonder when you have time to work).

When you finish listing, make a first draft of your resumé. If you have a computer and a word processing or page layout program like Microsoft Word or Pagemaker, producing an attractive resumé is fairly simple. And *simple* is definitely the integral word here. Unless you are applying for a job in a creative field like graphic design or advertising, it's best to err to the conservative. Less is more, leaving the jazzy elements behind. You do, however, want to make it quickly scannable by a hiring manager's eyes, and by a computer that will electronically scan the document. That means using plenty of white space, variations of type size, and some bold-faced type and bullets.

Today's resumés limit a lot of personal information that used to be standard. There truly is no need to list marital status or age, so don't worry that the separation will come up. In this litigious society, many employers prefer that you do not include this information. I also prefer a summary of skills and assets at the top of your resumé rather than an objective; an objective might needlessly disqualify you for a particular job.

Resumé writing requires a clear and tight writing style and effective use of action verbs. A potential employer will be impressed by your action. Wording phrases in the passive voice with "is, was, were" constructions doesn't give you the responsibility for your accomplishments. So brainstorm on yet another sheet of paper for appropriate action verbs or use the lists provided in resumé books.

The format you use is entirely subjective. Most formats work backwards, listing employment history and educational background from the most current position held. A functional resumé is best if you've worked on and off over the years. Shed as much positive light onto bad situations as possible.

Women concerned with a gap because they have been out of the workforce could call their document a professional briefing. Author Martin Yate told me this works best as you respond to classified ads or posted jobs. One side of the document lists the ad's requirements, and the other side showcases your qualifications that match. It's an innovative approach, but it should draw attention away from any employment gaps.

The same approach works for cover letters. Remember to use energetic language, not pompous prose. There is a line between taking responsibility and bragging. You definitely want to shine and have your self-confidence show through. Do focus on what you can offer the employer, not on what you like about them (at least until you've been asked this question in an interview).

Double-check and proofread obvious details such as the name of your contact and company, addresses, and other data. From the employer's point of view, if you can't get these details correct, what will you let slip by on the job? Make certain that your materials are printed well. A commercial printer is probably your best bet, but if you do print them on your computer's printer, make certain you have a good toner cartridge.

The length of your resumé and cover letter depends on several things. A younger woman's resumé won't demand the length that an experienced professional would at mid-life. Routinely, a resumé is best limited to two pages. I'd think long and hard before using three pages, unless you're applying for a high-powered executive position. If after two pages you still have more to include, you might try a stand-alone sheet of accomplishments. This might look better than a mammoth resumé.

Do be aware that headhunters, personnel officers, and others check facts and credentials. Thus there is a difference between highlighting responsibilities and inventing fiction. Don't go down this path, which will surely haunt you.

Exploring Your Career Options

Truly, your options are diverse as you determine a new career path or consider altering the one you've already established. With a prepared resumé in hand, or at least drafted, you have a clearer vision of your skills. You still might want to revise and polish that resumé to tailor it to a particular job or work arrangement.

Full-time work might best serve your needs, especially if you depend upon benefits. Given your particular profession, you may find it difficult to work a reduced schedule. I know of a friend who, due to companies going out of business, mergers, and the corporate transfer of her spouse, has treated each search for a full-time position as a job within itself. But she's succeeded, after literally hundreds of informational interviews. I've also heard that for each ten thousand dollars in salary, it may take that number of months to locate the ideal position.

Part-time employment does give you additional flexibility, and actually can come with benefits, depending upon the company. If you have young children who require your care, this might be an option that appeals to you. While economics might be a primary concern and motivation in finding a job, you must also look at quality-of-life issues. Does your attorney feel you are a candidate for alimony? If so, you may want to hold off on securing a hectic full-time position where you'll struggle to meet all of the family management tasks that fall to you.

One friend volunteered time in a school district that later offered her a part-time teaching position. Another established herself as a full-time employee, but later asked for a more flexible schedule with part-time hours. Because she'd proved her worth, she got the arrangement she requested.

Temporary employment is no longer synonymous with secretarial work. According to Peggy O'Connell Justice, who wrote *The Temp Track,* the temporary service industry now includes engineers, accountants, writers and editors, computer programmers, paralegals, managers and executives, as well as medical professionals. By working as a temporary employee, you get an inside perspective of the company you're assigned to. Here you can become a known quantity and prove your worth. You try out jobs and fields before committing to a contract, you gain experience and contacts, and you add to your resumé. The work is flexible enough that you can often choose when and where you work, for a day, a week, or several months. Temping allows you to learn from cutting-edge companies and leaders who are going places. Finally, signing up with an active temporary service provides fairly quick cash.

Look to the employment section of your Yellow Pages, or use the help-wanted ads or trade magazines to see which firms are in your area, and which specialize in placing one sort of professional over another.

Of course other alternatives are to telecommute or work from home in your own business venture. Perhaps you've always had the urge to be self-employed. A good idea ignites the entrepreneurial fire within a lot of women.

As I found researching *Working at Home While the Kids Are There, Too,* there are a myriad of paths you can follow to pursue entrepreneurial ambitions and still manage your family. Many women who are happy in full-time or part-time careers begin a venture on the side, moonlighting in a sense. Just don't let any visions of the perfect workplace cloud your judgment, for as convenient as working at home is, it has its struggles and perils. You'll be your own boss, set your own hours, dress the way you want, start and end the day when you want. No more traffic. No more putting up with people you'd just as soon ignore.

However, you'll have the temptation to slack off and the very real need to discipline yourself. Casual clothes can wreak havoc on your confidence; home workers jokingly call it "the slob factor." And there is isolation that leads to loneliness. If you have a hard time with discipline and deadlines, then explore telecommuting and work out of your home only on occasion.

Before you set out on a business venture, do realize there are risks that go along with the opportunities. Nothing takes the place of doing your homework and research.

Interviewing and Following Up

Entire books are written about acing the interview and being prepared for what a potential interviewer might ask you. Obviously you cannot memorize answers, but you want to come across as a professional with personality. Take the edge off that nervous feeling by being prepared and having knowledge of the company you interview with. Use your library and the resources in this chapter to prepare a short list of questions to ask.

Do dress appropriately, wearing conservative attire that's professional—not sexy. Leave the plunging necklines, flashy jewelry, black stockings, and stilettos in the closet (for future dates, of course).

During the interview, you may be asked some questions for which you don't have an easy answer. But you can be your own spin doctor. Why do you have limited experience? Reiterate that they won't find anyone willing to work as hard or learn as fast as you would, no matter how many candidates they interview. Dismissed from another position? Tell them you had fundamentally different views on what that job entailed. Why are you re-entering the workforce? Because you've had ample time to rethink your career and identify your own strengths and a new direction. Avoid saying, "I'm applying for this job because I'm separated and need the income." Everyone needs income.

And within a few days of the interview, do send a polite, handwritten thank-you note to the person who extended the courtesy of speaking with you. This cements a very favorable impression, and again puts your name in front of the decision makers.

Balancing the Professional with the Personal

How do you cope in the workplace when it seems the rest of your life is spinning out of control? This is a question many career women face as their personal lives are unraveling.

On one hand, you might be thankful for the distraction of having a job to look forward to and someplace to be each day. It sure beats burying yourself in legal battles and letting your mind fester with the escapades of your estranged. Then again, it's difficult to hide your emotions and set aside time to attend to legal and personal matters involving your separation.

Ask for flex time if your company offers this. Showing up an hour or two before the rest of the staff might give you more productive time, and an opportunity to work alone, without inquisitive coworkers. If you do feel on the brink of tears, go to the rest room for privacy or plan to take a long walk at lunchtime so you can have a good cry, get some fresh air, and exercise (which goes a long way to improving your mind's focus).

Don't make your boss your confidante in matters legal or personal. This just isn't a good idea, because some employers will think you are too preoccupied to attend to work. It's best to limit the calls you make or take regarding your case. Try grouping these together, if you must, during a time you are alone in the office and can talk. It's also wise to settle issues out of court whenever possible, or see if your attorney can represent you on matters not involving your presence. As I mentioned before, you're often paying for your attorney's time as she waits in the hallway before motions or hearings. And if you take time off, it doesn't help your career and/or bottom line.

Of course, it's impossible to think that your separation won't pop into your mind throughout the day. You can improve your spirits by removing pictures or mementos of your husband and family as it was. Place new photos on your desk, along with an inspirational or humorous calendar that's guaranteed to make you smile. Stock up on healthy snacks, hot cocoa, or anything else that's a treat during the workday so you can distract yourself as you start feeling down. Finally, enlist the help of a friend or an e-mail buddy who you can call occasionally or send messages to if your workload permits. Little sanity breaks like this go a long way.

Career-boosting Strategies

I'll bet there are some strategies you could implement to get noticed, get ahead, or get a raise. We'd all love that!

Only half of an author's job is actually committing words to paper. The other half is promoting projects, yes even ourselves. And since I've developed the idea of career-boosting strategies into a workshop I teach, I've also learned what's worked effectively for other professionals.

It's important to consider these possibilities because you want your peers, colleagues, and bosses to notice what you can offer and what you've achieved. This makes everyone happy. It places you in the mindset of other decision makers and potential employers. It even broadens your social circles. Sure, you need to be in the proverbial right place at the right time in many instances. But did you ever think that you can create those right times and places yourself? Well, you certainly can. Here are a few strategies to start you on your way:

- Keep your resumé current. You never know when it will be requested.
- Learn to be your own publicist. Make friends of the media, knowing which reporters cover your industry or field. An editorial or broadcast mention reaps plenty of rewards, much more so than paid advertising. The only investment is your time and talent. Just be sure you

honor a reporter's deadline, and even offer to help out if they ever need an expert sound bite from someone in your field.

- Practice word-of-mouth advertising. It starts with you! If no one is talking about what you're doing, then start telling others (within reason, of course). Ask your public relations office to release word of your promotions or accomplishments to local newspapers, or do this yourself. Ask satisfied clients or customers to tell their friends, family, or business associates about you. When you receive praise for a job well done, ask if you can use their endorsement if this is appropriate.
- Reward your referrals with thank-you notes, gift baskets, even tickets to events or performances if you can afford it. What comes around, goes around! Always mail a thank-you note after each interview you're granted.
- Offer to speak at school, charity, and professional venues. If you need to enhance your public speaking skills, join a group like Toastmasters. Then get out in front of groups like the Chamber of Commerce, a Rotary Club, alumni associations, and even bookstore gatherings.
- Teach a class. Even if you only know a bit more than others about your particular subject, it might be enough to help them and boost their perception of you. Lifelong learning and continuing education programs are always on the lookout for top-notch ideas and people to present them. Besides, it can yield additional income and contacts.

- Network. Then network some more. Though there are entire books written on the subject, you can begin doing this effectively by passing out plenty of business cards, writing notes to referrals, making full use of Internet newsgroups where people have questions, and offering to help others who may need a hand. After all, you never know when their stars will rise and remember your kindness.
- Dress for the job you want, not the job you have. Looking the part is pivotal.

Seven Steps to Higher Income

Even if you are happily employed, it pays to attract attention to your name and work. Nothing primes you for further opportunity like a solid reputation of excellent performance. Thus, pick up a few pointers here on how to get ahead in your chosen career.

1. Make yourself visible. Social extroversion is a predictor of higher income. Position yourself for a promotion. Champion your employment evaluations, showing how you've added to the bottom line. You just might see your numbers rise.
2. Become indispensable. Managers tend to give heftier raises to those they truly depend upon. Become one of those people by taking on projects that will reflect upon your boss as well as yourself.
3. Search for a new job, either in your current organization or in another. Trading up is the most significant way of increasing your salary potential.

4. Specialize and become the expert. Specialties exist in almost every career, and some are more lucrative than others. If necessary, obtain the required certification or additional degree to qualify for such status.
5. Change careers, even slightly. Moving your job title into a profit-performing part of the company can enhance your paycheck. Support positions generally pay less and don't offer bonuses and commissions like sales positions might.
6. Raise your prices if you're self-employed. Clients are unlikely to object to a reasonable price increase (say 5 to 10 percent) if you have a proven track record of satisfying their needs.
7. Negotiate a better benefits package. Whether it's better health or disability coverage, child care, free parking, tuition reimbursement, stock options, more vacation or sick time, or the ability to telecommute, each benefit translates into value.

You Go, Girl!

Think of this unplanned change as a turning point and an opportunity. Perhaps you have untapped potential and strength you're only beginning to realize. One day when I was suffering from bronchitis, I visited my physician's office. They asked if I'd mind if the resident assisting them took care of me. I didn't mind at all. In fact, I was inspired.

This woman was just a few years older than me. When I shared that I was a single mom, I discovered that she was also. After her divorce, she decided to go back to school and obtain her medical degree. Now there's accomplishment. And determination.

"A job can go a long way toward repairing the self-esteem that got bruised through the emotional rigors of the divorce process," writes Esther M. Berger, CFP, in *Money-Smart Divorce*. "And having a place to go every day and knowing that you earn your own paycheck can give you a tremendous sense of independence and self-worth."

Indeed, one woman I spoke with in my research dubbed work "the glue" that held her together during this difficult time. Her job forced her to get out of bed, look good, and get on with her life. At first she was timid, but her confidence grew and further opportunities came right along.

Remember, any career worth having takes time to build. Be willing to put yourself out there, to risk having your ideas and all that you offer rejected. It only takes one potential employer to say, "Yes, you're hired!" Develop the patience and tenacity to keep moving forward. Wake up every day with a "why not?" attitude. And whether you learn to speak in front of a group, write for professional or commercial publication, obtain another degree, or merely enhance the way in which you perform your job, keep improving your skills.

Chapter Eight

Household Hints and Car Care

When I faced the fact that my marriage was unraveling, I felt an onslaught of anger over many issues, not the least of which was the house we'd just built four years prior. We had purchased the property, saved diligently to pay it off, and then proceeded with what was to be our dream house. How could my husband have committed us to these responsibilities, then walk away, leaving me the burden?

Well, it doesn't matter where a husband's mind was when such events transpired. Fact is, you're separated, and in many cases, you have the family home to manage all on your own. Before you feel tempted to cry a bucket of tears or sell outright, let's put things into perspective.

It doesn't take massive amounts of testosterone to tend to the lawn, fix the dishwasher, or shop for a new car—a few of the concerns many of us might have handed over to the men in our lives. This chapter won't make you a car mechanic or a rival for Tim the Tool Man from "Home Improvement," but it will at least assuage the fear associated with everyday repairs and decisions. You'll learn a great deal, and transform burdensome tasks into manageable, perhaps enjoyable, ones. If nothing more, ladies, you'll discover the sheer exhilaration of power tools. Trust me, it's great therapy at times!

How You Can Be Handy

There were times I'd find something in the garage, hand it to my father, and ask, "What's this thing's purpose in life?" Once the garage became my domain, you wouldn't believe how many tools I discovered we owned and I never saw used.

It might be the same around your house. If you don't have dad or some other male friend to ask about items, take them to your local hardware store or browse the aisles for something that looks similar. Perhaps its purpose in life will make your life a lot easier. So put the tools you already own to the task.

Another way to ease the burden of managing home maintenance is to rely upon your feminine instincts. Ask questions. Women aren't afraid to ask questions. We adhere to the old adage that there is no stupid inquiry. We stop and ask for directions.

We also aren't so proud that we won't call in help when we're clearly into a task over our heads. Again, you'd be surprised how readily available household help can be. You merely need to know where to find the experts.

Perhaps there is a handyman in your neighborhood or church. Hire these fellas. In some cases, if they know you and the repair is minor, they might not even charge you. That's because many men love helping out a woman. It boosts their ego. So go ahead and ask.

Others who can lend a hand include the contractor who built your home (or the superintendent in an apartment building). You can find handymen and repair services through a chamber of commerce, Better Business Bureau, the Yellow Pages, local advertising supplements, or even your insurance agent.

Repair or Replace?

If funds are tight, replacing a worn-out appliance is the last thing you need. It's always a tough call. For instance, the washer breaks and the repair tech says it will cost $285 plus tax to get it spinning again. However, if you're willing to spend just under $600 you can buy a brand new one with a manufacturer's warranty. Unless an extended warranty already covers the expense, what do you do?

First determine the age of the appliance in question. Something that's under ten years old makes more sense to repair than its ancient counterpart. If you're dealing with hot water heaters, microwave ovens, or computers that are over twelve years old, seriously consider replacing them. These items just aren't made to last that long; computers that old are probably technologically outdated.

Next, look at the relative replacement cost and usage. It might take $2500 to replace your central air conditioning but only $800 to repair it. This would make sense to repair versus replace. Central air conditioning, refrigerators, ranges, and furnaces are big-ticket items you don't want to replace unless you absolutely must. And if you are considering a move, that's another reason to conserve cash and go with the repair. Furthermore, when an item qualifies as a business expense, the tax deduction may sway you. For computers and office equipment that boosts your bottom line, sometimes it takes money to make money.

Before you authorize a repair, ask if labor is charged by the hour or at a flat rate. If there is an estimate fee, make sure this is applied to any subsequent repairs. Always get a claim check with the company's name, address, and phone number, plus the technician's signature and your product's serial number. If your item is under warranty, be sure the receipt is marked "no charge." And ask for the replaced parts to ensure that the defective part was indeed replaced.

Household Maintenance Checklist

There are a number of household items that will last a lot longer with an ounce of prevention than if you hadn't tended to them. Here's a sampling:

- Heads or lenses of video equipment and audio components can easily be cleaned with the inexpensive cleaning units you can purchase.
- Dishwashers require hot water to dissolve soap. Thus, turn on the hot water before starting your dishwasher. Too much detergent causes etching on glassware. Rinse dishes before loading since food particles clog filters and impede water flow. Believe it or not, experts say dumping a jar of Tang into the dishwasher each month

and running it through a regular cycle cleans the dishwasher's parts by its acidic content.

- Clothes dryers need to be kept lint free. Wash the lint screen periodically with mild soap and water, and vacuum the vents and inside panels to prevent a fire hazard from forming from excess lint.
- Washing machines can be cleaned with two quarts of white vinegar poured into a machine full of hot water. Let it agitate for ten minutes, then let it sit for an hour before finishing the cycle. This cleans the buildup of lime, magnesium, and other deposits.
- Refrigerators are best served by vacuuming the condenser coils. Failing to do this can ruin the coils over time. Get a condenser brush, remove the front lower panel, and brush and vacuum the gunk. By unplugging the unit and removing the cardboard that protects the condenser coils, you can clean even more of the grime. It's best to do this once a year.
- Furnace filters and air-cleaning units should have filters replaced or cleaned annually. This improves efficiency and air quality.
- Defrost your freezer once ice accumulates a quarter of an inch.
- Unscrew drains periodically to clean out hair and soap that has accumulated. If your washer empties into a laundry tub, attach an old piece of pantyhose (use a rubber band to secure firmly). You'd be surprised how much lint this collects. Always use extreme caution when using liquid drain cleaners. Wear goggles and be certain not to breathe in the noxious vapors. A safer

alternative is the homemade mixture of one cup baking soda, one cup salt, and one-fourth cup cream of tartar. Shake this well in a jar and pour one-fourth cup directly down the drain, followed by two cups of boiling water. After letting it sit one minute, flush it out with cold tap water.

- Clear gutters in the spring and again in the late fall. Sometimes the window cleaning crew can do this.
- Hire a chimney sweep at least every few years to clean and inspect your chimney, sealing any cracks and insuring the safety of your fireplace.
- Apply a water sealant to your wooden decks or outdoor railings.
- Keep up with exterior painting tasks before the paint peels. Do this when weather permits and before harsh weather sets in.
- Conduct an energy audit (see Chapter 6) for tips on insulating, improving your home's energy efficiency, and saving money.
- Consult Chapter 5 for ways to secure your home properly.
- Prune shrubbery to keep it looking nice and growing well. If you don't own a hedge trimmer, you might be able to borrow one on occasion from a neighbor. Do use extreme caution if you aren't used to power tools. Install deer fence or other protective mesh so that the deer or rabbits don't feast on your rhododendrons or other plants.
- Cut off no more than one-third of the grass at a time. Scalping the lawn will weaken turf, cause it to burnout

and bring on disease. Use a mulching mower when possible. Never mow wet grass. It's bad for the lawn, the mower, and you.

Lessen that Lawn Art

Time to rev up the engine and mow that grass. A rite of springtime. And actually, a welcomed change after sitting indoors for months.

As a writer, I do my share of sitting, and much of my work might not see print for months, even years, after I've completed it. So lawn care, once I was suddenly single, became an outlet where I could immediately *see* the results of my labors. Only I had no idea what a creative outlet the results would be.

To start, I tackled the job like any good journalist would. Have a half-used bag of Scotts something-or-other. Call 800 number listed on the bag. Get that free booklet. Next step, e-mail a few male friends: "I know you're incredibly busy, so I've designed this survey with only one question, requiring a one-word answer. All right, at what age did you, all on your own, use a lawnmower?" Now I realize that this was a thoroughly whimsical, yet selfish approach. Instead of wondering when these two sons of mine could safely push the Black & Decker, I should have asked for bulleted lists complete with Power Point charts. Mistake number one.

This lapse was evened out soon enough. Another journalist's gem: Go to the experts (in this case, the guy in my neighborhood with the best lawn) and ask copious questions. Keep prying people until one of them tells you to go get a hobby.

Okay, for a while, all was just swell. It's amazing what sun and a little rain does to dirt. Then came mistake number two. I used that blasted spreader for the fertilizer application. It was painfully obvious that its previous owner hadn't taken care of it. Imagine pushing a rotary device that needed to be oiled—five years ago. But I wasn't smart enough to see my zebra lawn as being the spreader's fault. I still thought it was me.

In time, the stripes disappeared, but the lawn still had a few pesky weeds. On comes mistake number three. I got out *that* spreader, filled it, and pushed. And pulled. Pushed. And pulled. Cursing with each effort because it wasn't working well.

You pretty much have to live on my street to appreciate this, but within a week's time, there it was. Voila, lawn art. Patches and lines of brown in a pattern that only a two-year-old with a crayon might be able to depict.

One neighbor (a guy) smiled and asked if it was part of a writing assignment. Another (female friend) said no, I *had* to write about this. And the man with the great lawn? Well, he was too polite to comment. It was so horrendous that I just hoped no emergency would necessitate visits from family and friends afar. No, I didn't even want the minister to see this fiasco!

But what burns out and looks ugly has potential with that sun and rain factor. Throw on some topsoil and seed, and wait. And pray. Weeks later, when the growth appeared, I just shook my head. There were these psychedelic puffs of light green amid the blades of a more normal nature. Obviously, the turf color wasn't a great match!

Worse yet, they kept growing well into December, which leads me to tell you what no free booklet ever will. Lawn care ceases to be fun if you can't say good-bye to the task in October!

And for the mildly curious seeking a cheap thrill again this summer, don't worry. That spreader is now hopefully six feet deep. In the landfill!

Selling Your House?

If you're living in the marital residence that is jointly owned, you will need your estranged husband's cooperation to sell the property. But say you've been remarried, or you owned the home before your marriage. If the deed is still in your name, you're free to move if you choose.

With the other stress in your life, it's probably wise to use a real-estate agent. You'll be too preoccupied to list your house and deal with prospective buyers. Still, while you'll rely on your agent's advice, there are things you can do to hasten the sale of your home.

If you truly need to sell quickly, price your home realistically. Sure, you'd like to list it at the higher end of the fair-value range, but you'll get more traffic if you price it for quicker sale. The longer your house stays on the market, the lower its position becomes when agents punch up the computer printouts.

Do ask your agent if there is anything you can do to help. Certainly word-of-mouth advertising helps. When my husband and I tried to sell an apartment-sized condominium, I developed a flyer using my desktop publishing capabilities. It listed all the advantages our unit offered, with the incentive "why rent when you could own." Flyers can be distributed in apartment houses, libraries, and any other gathering spots that attract attention. Make sure your agent has a stack to hand out to interested buyers.

Make any cosmetic improvements you can afford. Repainting rooms to neutral colors and putting a fresh coat on the exterior lends curb appeal. So does keeping the lawn and shrubbery trimmed. Other subtle messages include setting a pitcher of lemonade on the patio set, arranging plants, having a fire in the fireplace, and simmering potpourri on the stove.

Fresh flowers are nice, and lots of light adds appeal. Set the kitchen or dining room table for a meal, or just have a bottle of wine, glasses, and napkins set out. This helps others visualize themselves entertaining or enjoying the home. Put out your best towels in the bathroom. Do keep pets outside, and try as best you can to clear closets and keep children's toys from view. Rent a storage locker if you must, at least while you are trying to show your home.

Car Shopping

When the time came to replace my ten-year-old car (appropriately dubbed "Schlep" among friends), I dreaded car shopping. That was until I realized that in all car purchases my husband and I had made together, I was always the one who haggled the price anyway.

Still, I had reason to be hesitant. I didn't know as much about cars as most guys did, and let's face it, who usually sells you your new set of wheels? Guys. So we women need to do our research before we're caught off guard or sold more than a car, but a line.

Try not to fall in love with what you picture as your ideal car. That is, don't be married to a make or model. (Having said that, your comfort level *is* important.) Reading is the best way to increase your auto knowledge and car-shopping prowess.

Call the National Highway Traffic Safety Administration for an informative brochure on buying a safer car. Dial 1-800-424-9393 and request operator assistance. Look up the annual *Consumer Reports* auto issue at your library or newsstand. This issue reviews current car models and gives buying tips. Besides, getting a feel for the repair records of used models is important even if you're buying a brand-new vehicle. *Edmund's New Car Prices & Reviews* gives invoice prices on new cars, trucks, and options. *The National Automobile Dealers Association (NADA) Used Car Guide* offers current trade-in and retail values. Borrow these resources at your local library. In addition, you can obtain the *Kelly Blue Book* value for automobiles you're buying or selling from your bank or directly off the Internet at www.kellybluebook.com.

This gives you plenty of information, but your thinking is far from over. Analyze your needs. Safety and reliability are obviously paramount. If you have children or other passengers (say you sell real estate), then four doors are necessary. If you use your car for work-related or recreational hauling, a spacious trunk or rack storage is handy. For those who live in a snowy climate, four-wheel or all-wheel drive helps, and if you traverse a hilly region you should consider a larger engine with six or eight cylinders.

Now that you have assessed what kind of car you need and can afford, next comes the actual shopping stage. Sure, you'll be visiting auto dealers, but you can also find vehicles at auction or from individuals you trust (so that you know the history of the car). In addition, call rental car companies to see if they are parting with any models. Then follow these tips:

- Don't buy based on monthly payments. Know the full cost. In fact, know what the dealer paid for the car (using the resources I named).
- Keep quiet about a trade-in, for dealers sometimes raise the price they quote you on the newer car. If you are trading in, figure this at the end.
- Consider where you will have the vehicle serviced but don't be swayed by this entirely. Should you find a model that your dealer/trusted garage doesn't sell, chances are good they can still service the car.
- Never take the first price you're quoted. Make the salesperson march back to the sales manager, several times if necessary. Get a written quote so they can't back out of it later. Hold your ground on your bottom-line price.
- Take any used vehicle to a third-party mechanic you trust. They'll look for signs of repainting, poor performance, and other red flags. Often for as little as $25, you can get a knowledgeable opinion. This small investment is comfort insurance that you've made a good decision.
- Make sure any money down is refundable, and get this in writing. Stipulate that the deal is contingent upon a successful outside inspection. Usually a dealer will only hold a vehicle for a few days this way, but it gives you time to investigate further.
- Remember that cash is king. If you can afford it, or if you've been saving to replace an older car, go ahead and

deal in cash—for two reasons. In your litigation, a large cash sum in the bank might be used against you. Secondly, you increase your bargaining power tremendously with a cash purchase.

- Realize that an extended warranty is one of the most expensive options you can tack on to the price, and it's a major source of profit for dealers. Therefore, don't allow yourself to be talked into options you do not need or want.
- Time your car purchase, if at all possible. Some say the best months to buy a car are the slow months of January through March. Others, however, swear that fall and into December are best. You might begin your research early in the month and conclude as you near the end when salespeople are eager to meet their quotas. The absolute best time to strike a deal is an hour before closing when the dealer is more willing to make a last-minute sale.
- Consider a "no haggle" model that many auto manufacturers have introduced if you truly can't fathom negotiating the price of a car.

Basic Car Care

If you used to defer all car-related matters to your husband, the responsibility of your automobile's maintenance now rests with you. A lot of us women also become accustomed to having a second car in the family (his car) to reply upon in emergencies. Now that you're separated, you probably don't have that steady back up plan.

For starters, revisit your insurance coverage. You may want to increase your deductibles on older cars, and take advantage of low-mileage discounts that could reduce your premiums. Since you don't want to be without transportation, inquire to see if your coverage has a rental car provision should your vehicle become involved in an accident.

Three immediate moves you should take are to (1) read your car's manual for suggested maintenance schedules and other tips (ask any dealer servicing your model for a schedule if you can't find yours); (2) enroll in an auto-care course especially designed for women; and (3) read *Lucille's Car Care,* written by transmission mechanic Lucille Treganowan and Gina Catanzarite. No joke, Lucille built her own successful repair shop, and her book includes everything from understanding the difference in oil labels and selecting a quality repair shop to emergency repair tactics and tips for your teenager's first car.

Keeping your car in top condition comes down to following a set schedule for such things as oil changes and other service. My mechanics always put a handy sticker on my windshield with the date and/or mileage at which I should have the oil changed next.

Have your mechanic rotate your tires every 5,000 miles for even wear (don't forget the full-sized spare if you have one), and always keep them properly inflated. Check the condition of your tires, replacing them when they reach 2/23-inch tread depth. When in doubt, use the penny test. Insert the top edge of a penny into the tread groove. If the top of the head shows, replace the tires. Replace belts on the recommended schedule, and get a tune-up also.

As Lucille says, you need to rely upon a sound-effects checklist and trust your common "scents." Listening for knocks and pinging is as important as looking for leaks, sniffing overheated elements, and inhaling a whiff of burnt rubber.

While you can always rely upon a trusted mechanic, you can learn to add windshield wiper fluid, test and add oil, and check antifreeze levels on your own. This is not rocket science.

Your Car's Emergency Kit

Pack the following in your trunk for emergency use:

- small throw rug for kneeling on and work gloves
- bread wrappers, rubber bands, roll of mechanic's wire
- large standard screwdriver, pliers, rubber hammer, and spray can of oil
- jumper cables and four-way tire wrench
- wheel chock, emergency flares, jug of water and a funnel
- flashlight, batteries, first-aid kit, blanket, nonperishable food (if stranded)
- old scarf, old belt, cigarette lighter, small shovel and some sand/cat litter

Defensive Driving

When I was first separated, I was amazed at how many people told me to be careful driving. It wasn't just my mom, mind you! I understood that friends and family were concerned about my safety on the highway.

Accidents easily occur when your mind is elsewhere. And let's face it, when you are emotionally upset, preoccupied by a dozen different details, groggy from sleepless nights, or adjusting to medication you might be taking, you and your passengers are at greater risk. Review this checklist just to be safe:

- Change car door locks or make certain you have all sets of keys your estranged husband may have had to your car. Again, don't let him rationalize that the car might be titled in his name also. Secure your vehicle.
- Consider a car security system or at least a steering wheel lock, particularly if your wheels are valuable, new, or one of the frequently stolen models (*Consumer Reports* often lists these annually).
- Become an auto club member (AAA) for added security. If you ever break down, you can call the number and receive free or discounted towing within the vicinity.
- Consider purchasing a cellular phone for emergency calls (see below).
- If you live in snow belt states, stash emergency items in your trunk. These items include a small shovel, chains (if you use them), salt, kitty litter or sand for added traction, a flashlight (that works!), an ice scraper and snow brush, jumper cables, work gloves, white rags, flares, extra wiper fluid, and blankets, food, and water should you become stranded.
- Keep at least a half tank of gas in your car at all times.
- Use caution. Sure, you'll probably be frazzled for a while and chronically short for time. But don't hurry,

especially when you could harm yourself, your children, or innocent others in an accident.

Selecting a Cellular Phone

According to *Consumer Reports,* the majority of cellular telephone owners have their phones for safety's sake. Anyone stranded on the highway can benefit from having a mobile phone, especially women who might be less willing to change a flat tire or tackle some other car repair.

If you're unfamiliar with cellular phone service, start with a plan that doesn't require a long-term commitment and one that carries no early termination penalty should you decide to opt out of the service.

Currently, there are three types of phones on the market—analog, digital, and personal communications services (PCS). PCS phones offer a little more security from eavesdropping, but an older analog model might suffice for emergency use only. The phone itself might be less expensive, but the air time is costlier. Digital phones offer better sound quality and lower air time rates. If your needs for a phone extend to the business uses of faxing, voice mail, caller ID, and Internet use, then PCS is probably your best bet. Fancier handsets aren't guaranteed to work with another carrier if you switch service, so stick with something plainer and more universal.

When shopping for the whole package of phone and service, freebies might look good, but beware. They can lure you with the promise of free air time or a free phone, but you're probably paying for those items somewhere in your contract.

Ask your provider to show you a map of its coverage area, and then determine if this suits your needs.

Cellular phone thieves listen for people to give their credit card numbers and other privileged information over the air. Also, be conservative about who you give your cellular number to. You have the phone for your convenience and safety, but if others use it indiscriminately, you'll be the one charged. If your estranged husband is the vindictive type, you might be wise to keep the number from him.

Chapter Nine

Learning to Lighten Up

Right when I faced several unpleasant realities about my marriage, my minister gave a thoroughly inspirational sermon one Sunday. In relating how we all walk difficult paths, including those of separation and divorce, he came to the conclusion that "you can become bitter, or you can get better."

No doubt about it. A marital separation, especially when you least expect it, ranks up there as a horrendous life passage. I can now look back at those first few months, even years, and see that I was angry. I harbored a lot of negative energy. I had every right to feel anger as well as every other negative emotion in the dictionary. And so do you. But you also need to learn to let it go.

This chapter is about letting out the anger and allowing in the laughter that may be sorely lacking from your spirit. In what I hope is lighthearted text, I'll relate incidents many women have shared with me, all true and all too grand not to laugh at. That's the whole point here—learning to laugh again.

Bitter vs. Better

So how do you know what qualifies as bitterness and when to know you're getting better? Truth is, you won't always know the distinction. This is a very subjective matter. Time helps to tell you. So might friends who can see things a little more objectively.

For instance, your take on the following story will most likely reflect where you are in the journey of your separation and/or divorce. One woman struggled since her husband ran off with his coworker. She ran into another jilted woman at her daughter's school, and the two got to talking about these "other women."

Now, every time she feels the betrayal, the anger, the hurt, she focuses on one profound, perhaps funny thought. During her chat at the school, the new friend she'd made summed up the situation.

"Let's call these other women what they really are," new friend shared. "Bimbos."

Now, this scenario may make you think these women weren't letting go. But in a sense they were. Friends have certainly added even more pejorative terms to my vocabulary, and I think any female facing infidelity can relate to the word these two women laughed at. And, I don't think it's bitterness unless it's a constant state of mind (rather than an occasional laugh).

When you're with trusted friends or those you know can empathize, let go of a little propriety. Yes, call that other woman a bimbo behind her back, or tell your best friend how happy you are that the bottom feeder you used to live with swims in someone else's aquarium. Whatever! Unless you wake each day breathing fire, unless you air these sentiments in front of your children, or unless you harbor meanness, an occasional verbal stab among friends can elicit a good laugh.

Why Move On?

I placed this chapter toward the end of the book on purpose, because as you progress through the weeks and months of your separation, you'll find it easier, as I did, to move on. And if you think it's not even a conceivable goal, then realize the alternatives—a life of bitterness, anger, and depression. Furthermore, think of the effect on your children.

In collaborating with my friend, psychologist, and author, Dr. Timothy F. Murphy, I've learned a lot about anger's power and the reasons to rein it in. Dr. Murphy and I have written *The Angry Child*.

Tim has shared with me that in all his years of practice, the moments he most wanted to pull a parent aside and lay into them a little has been over issues of divorce and its effect upon the children involved. Most therapists probably would love to shout, "Grow Up!" because many divorcing people are blind to their own anger and emotions. So the lesson here for you, as an individual and as a parent, is to try as hard as you possibly can to manage your emotions, purge the anger in a positive way, and accept a new direction in life. Even if you don't want to. If you're like me, you'll realize that while you never anticipated this passage, you have become stronger, and you'll continue to be.

Reframing Your Past

Another friend was employed as a therapist years ago. When I get a little down about what's transpired, I count on her for a quick reframing lesson.

Reframing occurs when we take a scenario that looks bleak and unappealing and shed new light on the picture. We can choose to wallow in uncertainty and hurt, or we can move to higher ground and a brighter outlook.

So regardless of who initiated your separation, you've had to cope to preserve your sanity and survival. Sure, you might have additional responsibilities, loneliness, and mixed emotions. But look at it this way. The bathrooms probably aren't as dirty, the food lasts longer, and the laundry might be a genuine snap. And if you have children, sure you must continue to wrangle with the father, and yes, you'll miss the kids when they're with him. But visitation can also equal time to lounge in bed on Saturday morning, time to date, or moments merely for yourself.

I'm not saying reframing your situation will be easy. Far from it. What has happened in your marriage is history, and I know the temptation well to beat yourself up about what transpired. Could you have seen signs of trouble? Probably not, from where you were standing at the time. Even if the wife in us may have had an inkling, the mother in us was most likely steadfast in wanting to make the family unit work. I know I had two children that required extra efforts. I could have used help. I understand *exactly* how you might feel trying to salvage a bad situation.

Frankly, meeting the needs of children with special concerns is taxing. I really feel for women who are left with primary responsibility of mentally handicapped, chronically ill, or physically challenged children because another set of adult hands in the home is such a relief. I've aligned dozens of doctors, physical therapists, speech clinicians, school nurses and counselors, plus teachers over the years to team with me in helping my children. That's a lot of juggling, and a lot of phone calls, driving to appointments, and believe me, a lot of paperwork.

However, it's my ability to find the pride, joy, and accomplishment in this responsibility that allows me to reframe. I have made things happen for these two boys. My priorities were and still are right. People I've met, even men I've dated, tell me I'm doing a great job. My children are indeed my two greatest accomplishments, and I choose to focus on this whenever the other negative stuff starts to pull me down.

I hope you'll join me in learning to look at the cheerier side of things. I'm not dismissing your circumstances or making light of them. I know what it's like to be devastated, afraid, lonely, troubled, and then some. From here on out, however, I'll take a much more humorous tone. At times it might be sarcastic, occasionally flippant. But these are all coping mechanisms as we heal. And heal we must.

A Heavy Heart Isn't Healthy

If you listen to the experts, you'll realize that lightening up aids more than our mental health. Published studies indicate that wealth doesn't really buy true happiness. It only tips the scale ever so slightly above the satisfaction level of the average American. So what, then, has the power to make us happy, and healthy?

Norman Cousins, who wrote the book *Anatomy of an Illness,* details recovery from pain and terminal illness using humor therapy. Laughter not only reduces muscle tension, but it also stimulates the heart and lungs. When we laugh, we give our bodies the same benefit that a deep breath allows, increasing the oxygen levels in our bloodstream. We raise our endorphin level, and we increase the number of disease-fighting antibodies. That's why chronically depressed people are often the sickest people. Sure, they have a virus or a disease that has struck them, but their mood certainly hasn't helped their health.

Some experts have theorized that we are born destined to be happier or sadder based upon our genetic makeup. But even if this is so, we can often adjust our contentment level by acknowledging what gets us down and keeps us happy. We can steer clear of the former and lean toward the latter.

Life is indeed filled with obstacles. That's a given. How we deal with these openly determines the satisfaction we derive out of life. Others who have written about the habits of happy people note that most contented individuals think highly of themselves. Thus, they have higher self-esteem. Happy people tend to feel in control of their lives. Right now, you may still feel that your future is out of control, perhaps even at the whim of the court. But this will get better, and indeed you can exercise greater control over day-to-day details of even small segments of your life.

Perky people tend to be optimistic as well as extroverted. If you find yourself battling pessimism, a good cognitive therapist may help you reframe matters. Marc Meyers shares tips in *How To Make Luck: Seven Secrets Lucky People Use To Succeed*. He says to limit your relationships with negative people, a surefire way to push away pessimism. Brainstorming for mood elevators is another tactic. Music, he says, can be upbeat in more ways than one. If you're trying to become more extroverted, use the healing power of the pen to help you get there.

Finally, you can make yourself happier by filling your life with laughter. Former *Good Morning America* host Joan Lunden, herself a survivor of separation and divorce, chronicles her own laugh track in her best-seller *A Bend In The Road Is Not The End Of The Road*. After interviewing an expert on trauma and grief counseling, Lunden learned that it takes three to five years to fully recover from divorce and even begin to think about rejoining life. Lunden writes, "When we can no longer change a situation, we are challenged to change ourselves."

Joan is right. Change frightens us all, and one of the best action strategies she presents is to write down whatever it is that scares you or causes you to feel negative. Then write the complete opposite. For instance, she says, write "change is scary" followed by "change is exciting." To follow up this exercise, Lunden suggests that you continually remind yourself of these positive thoughts. Put sticky notes on your mirrors and bulletin boards. Do this and you'll fill your mind with warm, wonderful images as opposed to the old ones that got you so down and depressed.

Developing Happy Habits

What makes one woman happy might make another miserable. That's life. It's entirely subjective. Nonetheless, there are additional remedies to swing your mood in a more positive direction.

For starters, know what *not* to do. This includes obsessing and ruminating, which we women tend to do. Try not to spend excessive time thinking about the husband who walked out the door. The more you think of and discuss this man and what impact he's had on your life, the more connected you will feel to him. Thus, the more controlled you'll continue to be by *his* actions, not your own.

Instead of coming home to an empty house or apartment, get yourself out among people. It's a lot harder to sit and think about unpleasant events when surrounded by other people, their conversations, and their distractions. It's also a great way to meet new friends so that, again, you aren't reminded of what you did as a couple. You begin to redefine yourself as a single woman with a bright future.

Treat yourself to a restaurant meal. I know it's not easy to take yourself out for dinner, but do it. Who cares if others look at you in the booth with your book? It's a meal you don't have to cook, scenery different from your own four walls, and at the very least, a diversion. Someone else might not have treated you well, but you can darn well give yourself permission to treat yourself like a queen if you see fit.

Journaling your way to happiness, you'll learn that list making is a helpful endeavor. Create a list of things you've always wanted to do but never did fit into your married lifestyle. Maybe it's taking up ceramics or enrolling in a writing class. For me, I'd always wanted to learn more about investing money, and I needed to develop a Web page to promote my books. Noncredit, lifelong-learning classes provided insights and new interests.

If you don't reorganize your life, you'll continue to feel your spouse's absence, or that of your children, if they live now with their father. Volunteer commitments are wonderful opportunities to give to worthwhile organizations at a time in your life when you feel least able to write a check. During my separation, I joined the crusade to educate others about and eradicate domestic violence. A very courageous family in my community lost their daughter in a domestic violence standoff. They turned their grief into good by establishing a task force that visited schools, put up displays, marched in parades, met with law enforcement officials, and ultimately worked to create a safe house for women and children in their first few days fleeing abuse. I lent my writing talents to help with brochures and written material, even putting domestic violence links on my own Web site.

Writing Your Own Prescription

A separation brings overwhelming emotions. Writing your own prescription may be the answer. Professional therapists as well as authors extol the virtues of journaling. *In The Meantime* author Iyanla Vanzant says, "Write out what you fear, what you think could happen, what you would feel if that happened, what would happen to you if that happened, and anything else you can think of that keeps you in fear. End this exercise by writing, 'I do not choose to have this experience. I choose to _____.' Complete the sentence by writing out what you want."

Uncovering emotions is why the majority of patients seek professional therapy. Writing is often used as an adjunct because it integrates the body and the mind. For instance, eating disorder patients report past traumatic experiences associated with food. Journaling brings about awareness. It also puts distance between the writer and the problems people struggle with, allowing them to see multiple facets until a new perspective emerges.

To begin a journal, try list making, which seems to be the latest trend in self-analysis. In this age where some health-care plans lack mental health coverage, writing is a first resort for many people. Lay people have dubbed the phenomenon "scriptotherapy." As people make lists as part of their writing exercises, what was once painful writing can become a list of blessings, as if they are looking at life through a gratitude lens. It's all in how you look at things.

Experts also credit writing with lowering inhibitions and alleviating stress-related diseases. The National Science Foundation and National Institutes of Health funded research by James W. Pennebaker, Ph.D., who found that people who wrote about their deepest feelings evidenced heightened and persistent immune function. Pennebaker described his research in *Opening Up: The Healing Power of Expressing Emotions*.

Of course, writing includes other genres besides journaling and list making. There's the letter you never send or the imaginary conversation you have between yourself and your worst enemy (gee, who might that be?). Just be aware that while the written word can be cathartic, it can also lead to obsessive rumination, impeding any therapeutic goal you hope to achieve. It's never a substitute for a friend or a therapist if you're truly troubled.

Start your journal when it's quiet and you're relaxed. Instrumental music does help the creative spirit. So does setting aside a block of time, say fifteen minutes a day. Date your journal entries so that you can chart your progress, your chronicle of events, or your reflections as you overcome difficult moments.

As an author, I've obviously found that my profession has the power to help me heal or purge thoughts. Very shortly into my separation, I realized the need to economize even more than I'd always done. My frugal nature had never bothered me until I suppose I was forced to make financial cuts. For whatever reason, I felt a little sad at accepting help or having to make financial adjustments. So I put my thoughts on the subject of saving, being frugal, and how society looks at thrift on paper. Very soon, it was *in* the paper, as the *Pittsburgh Post-Gazette* ran my piece. I'd shared what it was like growing up with my dad, known for his trash finds whereby he'd rescue something he saw along the side of the road and fix it up for one of us to use. I talked about having Depression-era parents and how that can be a good thing in today's "gotta have it now" society. Well, not only did writing this column lift my spirits, but it provided much of Pittsburgh with a little laugh as well, I'm told.

Lessons in Lightening Up

I still remember the time I was lamenting to a friend that my computer printer died — a travesty to us writers! I was telling her that my estranged husband seemed surprised I replaced it so quickly since I'd always deferred to his guidance on computer matters.

"Loriann, you don't get it," my friend told me. "You're supposed to be lying at the bottom of the steps begging him to come back. But the house is still standing, the lawn isn't three feet, and by God, you did the ultimate – you went out and got computer literate." This newfound independence brings to mind another lighter moment—observations my husband made during the holiday season. First, he wondered who put up the Christmas lights (as well as the deer fence protecting the shrubbery). Weeks later, we got together for the boys' gift exchange. When I gave him some of my traditional rum balls, he seemed surprised I'd even made them.

Well, who'd he think put up the lights and deer fence—the elves? I did, and I told him as much, ignoring the stunned look on his face. As for the rum balls, I did all the work on these most other years, so why would I break tradition?

Honestly, I think many men believe wives will just shrivel up and die without them. Hello! We have lives. We have interests. We have traditions. Husband or no husband, life goes on.

All right. You get the idea of what it takes to lighten up, even if it's between you and your friends. Again, I'm not suggesting that you try these tactics out on your estranged. Certainly anything you put into writing can and probably will be used against you. Just learn to reframe things, making jokes out of even the worst scenario, and you will feel your body and mind relax.

Seriously though, I believe that many men (especially control freaks) define themselves through their interactions with spouses. Without their wives to push around, they are nothing. If this fits the description of your interactions, merely refuse to play the game. Set limits. Demand to be treated well. Hang up the phone if you must. I'm always amazed by men who can't control their rage, particularly on the telephone. You'd think these guys would have grown nodules on their vocal cords by now from screaming. It's hard to figure them out. But alas, I don't believe the Environmental Protection Agency has declared good single men an endangered species. At least not yet!

If It Acts Stupid, It Probably Is Stupid

Wasn't there a line in *Forrest Gump* that said something about "stupid is as stupid does?" Well, plenty of estranged husbands make some absolutely bonehead moves. Honestly. Instead of asking their doctors to write a script for Viagra, these guys need brain-potency pharmaceuticals.

In researching this book, I collected many stories. And each woman has a gem to tell. One husband, upon separating, promised to live cheaply with soup and canned goods. So his wife helped him pack up pots and pans (old ones mind you!), and she threw in a can opener. "Gee, I hadn't thought of that," the guy remarked.

The next guy attended his son's school play. He knew his estranged wife would also be there each night they performed because their son had a lead role. Each performance, Studly walked in with a different woman on his arm. Finally, one of the wife's friends shook her head and said, "What's WITH him? Can't he even get a second date?"

Another man called his estranged wife at six o'clock while she and the kids were trying to eat dinner. He greeted her with, "Would you like to save money?" She thought he was a telemarketer, and hung up.

In my own separation, I needed to replace my ten-year-old car. My husband refused to sign the title for a trade-in. But I'd found exactly what I needed, and fortunately that save-for-a-rainy-day mode served me well. I just went out and bought what I wanted before it got snapped up. Of course, my little one spilled the beans to his dad one night. Oh how I wish I could have been there to see his face when he was told "mommy got a new car." I'd have added, "You didn't REALLY think I thought you'd sign that title, did you?"

One woman's cheating ex-husband got a promotion, a post that demanded his presence all over the globe. During an exchange he prided himself over his jet setting. "Aren't you sorry you didn't stick with me?" he asked. She was thinking, "I'd rather go to Alcatraz with a faithful guy than Australia with a louse who hasn't a clue what monogamy means."

Another man insisted on a separation despite the pleas of his wife and children to stay put. He claimed he needed peace and quiet, but the room he rented was next door to a fast-food drive-thru. Each morning and late into the night he was awakened with, "Would you like fries with that?"

And even if your marriage was a rocky road, there will come a time when another man shares your life. You'll get to savor the moment when your ex meets Mr. Right. It's only human nature to enjoy this a little bit. One woman dubbed this meeting the "who the hell are you moment," because indeed that's what her ex belted out seeing her new beau reading the newspaper, sipping a martini, and sitting in his old chair!

Being Better Off

Sooner or later, women facing divorce learn to look at their future with a positive glow. At first, the one-phrase sentences outsiders offer may make you even angrier. "He wasn't your type anyway" or "You'll be better off without him." These lines sound trite. Indeed they probably are, because in many cases, the people trying to cheer you have never ventured down this path themselves.

So I asked women who have taken the journey. Here are some thoughts, mixed with my own, when I asked them to complete the phrase "you know you're better off divorced when . . . "

- You find yourself exploring your hobbies, not his.
- You can forget which night Al Michaels hosts football.
- Your basement isn't a graveyard of broken gadgets, rusted tools, or thingamajigs.
- Your mother can visit anytime.
- Your garden consists of rosemary and lavender rather than beefsteak tomatoes and jalapeno peppers.
- It's goodbye deer hunting and trout fishing. Hello art classes and book discussions.
- You don't have to deal with dirty socks, discarded underwear, or his mother.
- Your food lasts longer, costs less, and means half the work.
- Each day brings a little victory versus a defeat.

After reading that list, go ahead and display your old Barbie collection on the mantel. Talk to your girlfriends on the phone all night long, or like me, keep the TV tuned to CNN. Spend Super Bowl Sunday at the ballet. One woman reported how blissful it was to enjoy a night out that didn't involve wings, beer, and Hooters! Commandeer the recliner, the remote control, and the hot water supply.

Have you ever rolled your eyes at your coffee table magazine collection that rivals the waiting room of a urologist's office? Well, deep six the swimsuit issue and stock up on *Martha Stewart's Living* if you want.

Freeze the lasagna leftovers, and sneak a few pieces of the kids' Halloween candy. When you go on trips, near or far, you pick the destination, and get this. You'll know you're better off divorced when you don't have to ask for *his* directions, and frankly, you don't even care if he's lost on his journeys. You'll travel your way—the whole way—and you'll know where you're going from the get-go!

Finally, view his midlife crisis as your opportunity. Taking the higher ground is so much more pleasant than his dirt path, in many respects. Say something breaks. Hire a handyman, albeit a handsome handyman, to fix it. Okay, if that's not in the budget, try fixing it yourself for we women can often do more with a can of WD-40 than he ever did with his entire toolbox. Another thing about being in charge of repairs is that you can discover the sheer exhilaration of power tools. And, isn't it nice when there's no engineering treatise offered over the most mundane snafu.

Man watching is a wonderful way to pass the time. Dating can also be fun. Men can be both supportive and friendly. And, sex is even more sensational the second time around when you know you're loved and respected for who you are.

When it's all over, and the legal papers are filed away, the only person you'll seek to improve is yourself. And if you have children, all of your decisions from this day on focus on your—and their bright future. It will shine. And so can you!

Having the Last Laugh

Indeed, few people emerge unscathed from a separation and divorce. It takes a bit of moxie to brush yourself off and steam forward. But good things can result.

Remember that choosing to be lighthearted doesn't mean you don't care about the difficult path you've walked, nor does it make that path fade into the landscape. If you lead with a lighthearted approach you make the conscious choice to be empowered by all of your struggle and survival. This alone will carry you during the days ahead. And when life gets you feeling low or your estranged lives up to the strange component of that word, just say to yourself, "Well, there's something to be said for consistency!"

Chapter Ten

Exploring New Horizons

So you've come to the last chapter in this book. For you, decisions might be determined already, or you may still ponder what path to take. Some marriages surviving separation will reconcile, and this possibility should not only be explored but celebrated if the two of you can grow from what has gone wrong. Hopefully, the individual counseling you may have received has helped you determine whether reconciliation would be a positive step forward versus a halting step back.

In other separations, it's clear that the marriage will end in divorce. This might result because one of you has made the choice and informed the other. In cases where behavior is not corrected, is denied, or is indeed dangerous (domestic abuse or serial infidelity), then divorce becomes necessary. Take the philandering husband who can't control his behavior yet wants the happy family façade. Most women would agree that he can't have both.

Even if divorce results against your will, what lies ahead can indeed be exciting. Sure, there are bound to be changes, some loneliness, and other adjustments, but in time you can learn to see these as opportunities, not setbacks. For instance, facing the newly single crowd can be daunting, but it can also be fun, leading you to new activities and friendships.

Lingering Questions

If you're still undecided about which direction your marriage should take, there is a book that may help. *Should You Leave* by Peter D. Kramer, the psychiatrist who brought us *Listening to Prozac,* explores personal autonomy versus interpersonal intimacy, and the question of whether to stick out a troubled relationship. It's got good information. Kramer writes, "When you ask whether you should leave, what is at issue includes fairness. Is it disloyal for you to bow out? Is the commitment made to you being honored? Are you being taken advantage of? Is an isolated instance of betrayal a sign of abuse, or is there a level at which your partner remains trustworthy? Is your implicit bargain corrupt or honest?"

Those are the questions you will have to face when you decide to reconcile or divorce. If there is blaming or refusal to change a major issue (like infidelity or abuse), is the marriage worth saving? Or does the quick escape route (usually another partner) look particularly appealing? Most people mistakenly think that a quick flight into another nest will solve their problems. "Not so," say the experts. If you don't deal with your difficulties now, they will haunt you in other relationships.

Nothing says you must answer these questions immediately, for marital separations sometimes last many years until the parties have compelling reasons to move beyond them. Time has a way of showing us our path. The goal is to arrive at a new contract that works for you.

Attempting a Reconciliation

Remember the famous Ann Landers' question: Are you better off with him, or without him? There are some unions where escape is simply the easy out, and in all sincerity, you might be better trying to save the relationship.

I have seen marriages put back together. In fact, 80 percent of all married couples separate for at least two months. In addition, 18 percent of all couples that divorce remarry each other. For those couples, a separation is used as a marital time out, a chance to reflect upon your problems, feelings, and goals. It's easy to run right back to the marriage out of fear. Few of us want to be alone, and no one looks forward to single parenting or financial adjustments. However, if you reconcile prematurely, you risk splitting up permanently, and those are the adjustments you will indeed make.

Hopefully, you have sought your own therapy. When domestic abuse or a partner's affair has shaken your self-esteem, it's even more necessary to find individual counseling. Assuming it's safe and wise to contemplate getting back together, your next step will most likely be marriage therapy.

A trained counselor can help you realize the distorted thinking patterns that may have led to misunderstandings and hurt feelings. All relationships go through phases, and all have some conflict. It's a matter of how you handle that conflict, and how you strive for equality in the marriage. Communication and conflict resolution are skills that can be acquired.

Counseling can also help determine your list of emotional needs. Everyone has them. In fact, couples who make a point of meeting their partner's top five needs stand a better chance of building a healthier marriage. Even focusing on the top two puts you ahead of the game. Truly when our emotional concerns go unmet, we tend to feel empty, and we're willing to sacrifice just about anything to have them met, even our spouses, children, careers, or core beliefs.

Many pop-psychology books give lists of typical man and woman needs. For instance, most men give highest priority to sexual fulfillment, recreational companionship, physical attractiveness, domestic support, and admiration. Women, on the other hand, rank their top needs as affection, conversation, honesty and openness, financial support, and family commitment. The only way you'll know your husband's needs is to ask. And the same goes for him. As adults we are responsible for understanding our own feelings, integrating that knowledge for useful purposes, and indeed communicating that perspective to our spouse.

PERFECT TIMING

It takes time to meet each other's needs so don't expect overnight success. Most important, it takes time alone, time without friends or family (including your own children), and time that's truly earmarked for attention, as you did when you first dated and fell in love.

Time was a shortcoming in my own marriage. Though I'm sure there were moments where I could have made myself more available, I felt I had to fight hard for time alone with my husband. There was enormous pressure to vacation with extended family, and there weren't many child-care options available for a real reprieve. Even after the toughest year of our marriage, when we'd brought our preemie infant to relative health, I was reprimanded by his family because I'd planned a week long escape for the four of us. Certain wrong assumptions must have been made about our priorities, and that stung. To this day, I'm jealous of those couples who escape together with relative ease (and relative support!).

That vacation we took, ironically a year before we separated, did wonders to renew us as a family and rekindle romance. My husband's coworkers even urged me to take him away again because they'd never seen him so relaxed. Even though we ultimately divorced, I do know the power of a reprieve. If you can't leave the children behind, choose a vacation with excellent child care. Boscobel Beach, a SuperClubs resort in Jamaica, the Disney Cruise Line, or the Big Red Boat are all examples of vacations where couples can delight in one another while making sure their children are happy and safe on the premises. Search for a vacation option that appeals to your needs and budget. Just be certain there is group childcare for your time alone.

To really reconcile your differences, of course, other tasks need to occur, but these can't happen unless you dedicate those precious moments. Spending time with a spouse shows him, or shows you, that there is respect, especially if you are overcoming infidelity. A woman who doesn't feel respected out of the bedroom will rarely feel that way in it. Time also affords us the chance to actively listen, paraphrase back to our partners what we've heard, and make sincere attempts at two-way communication. Time gives us the opportunity to learn new things together—to take a class, become familiar with our partner's favorite pastimes, or merely make new memories. Taking even a minute here or five there allows us to have fun, for it only takes a second to scribble a funny note tucked inside a briefcase, send a sexy e-mail or pager message, or reach out to offer a much-needed hug.

OTHER STEPS

The other necessary ingredient toward successful reconciliation is an open mind. You need to be able to understand the world as your partner sees it. This doesn't mean you necessarily must agree with it, just take that emotional leap.

How often have you looked objectively at a friend's marriage and wanted to shake her into reality? Perhaps she has what you yearn for, only she stubbornly refuses to make minor changes. Sure you don't walk in her shoes, and you don't want to coerce her into something she's personally uncomfortable with. But I'm talking little things here—like being open to new recreational pursuits, taking a different kind of trip, engaging in playful conversation if there has been too serious a stance, or even splurging for Victoria's Secret merchandise when she's shunned it before. Again, the way to determine which changes—minor or major—in your attitude require focus is to ask your spouse and consider the possibilities with an open mind. The results might just surprise you.

Finally, it's essential that you learn the language of reconciliation. To succeed at setting new expectations and negotiating your differences, you must overcome the anger and resentment that led you to separate in the first place. One step to take in removing the negativity from your life is to eliminate it from your speech and tone of voice. For instance, which request sounds easier to acquiesce to?

"Don't put the dishes in the rack that way." Or

"When you load the dishwasher, could you please be careful not to bang the dishes."

For starters, the first sentence is demanding and negative. The second states your request in the positive and adds a little information that goes a long way in explaining your meaning, and ultimately getting cooperation with the dishes. Thus, eliminate negative constructions that begin with don't or never. In essence, learn to treat others as you'd like to be treated yourself.

Overcoming Infidelity

When spouses promise to be sexually and emotionally faithful, and then aren't, the betrayal is wrenching. Often if you can understand why the infidelity occurred, you feel more in control. It's when there are no clear answers that confusion reigns, and it is harder to overcome.

Of course, we've all heard the definitions of what constitutes sex, let alone infidelity. My feeling is: If in doubt, ask your spouse if it constitutes infidelity. Of course, some jealous partners consider flirting as being unfaithful, but if the excitement of a crush is transferred to the marriage, then you might be thankful for it. *Psychology Today* in August, 1998, ran a cover story on overcoming infidelity during the Monica Lewinsky scandal. It pointed out that if unfaithful partners treated their spouses the way they approached their lovers, the spouses would probably be ecstatic. The report also concluded that yes, oral sex counts; infidelity is more serious the earlier it occurs in a marriage; and if you think you were unfaithful because you weren't getting enough in the marriage, you probably weren't giving enough to begin with.

If you've been the spouse who was cheated on, then you know the trauma. You'll act a little crazy, almost hypervigilant, until you can start to manage the scar tissue that's resulted in the relationship.

If you're the spouse who did the cheating, realize that your husband will feel that everything has been a lie. Your marriage has lost its innocence. In fact, the deceit is sometimes harder to bear than the actual sexual images. Traitors who commit treason against their country have been sentenced to death. In the minds of most betrayed spouses, that seems too mild a punishment to fit the crime.

Oh, there will be anger. And the hurt will run deep. Occasionally, the debt is too big to pay off. But some woman will likely overlook the transgressions, giving the husband a second chance. Will that woman be you?

The betrayer also goes through an emotional gamut, feeling ashamed, guilty, anxious about adverse consequences (loss of reputation, job, income, assets, children). Personally, I don't have much sympathy for betrayers who compound secrets because they don't want to deal with the destruction left behind. With disclosure, there can be hope. With secrets, there is shame.

I firmly believe there is no excuse for infidelity. Therefore, you shouldn't blame yourself if you're the victim. One husband rationalized that by hiring hookers he never forced anyone, as if that made up for breaking his vows, lying to his wife, risking everyone's health, and quite possibly corrupting minors (since many prostitutes are runaway teens).

Some betrayals are deliberate attempts to hurt the innocent spouse, and many others are committed to avoid intimacy. By placing one's attention and energy outside the marriage, one runs away from emotional involvement of the family instead of dealing with it. When this happens, infidelity serves as a barometer to say something else is wrong with the person seeking escape. Does this sound like you or your estranged?

Though it's the common perception that infidelity is all about sex, it rarely originates there. In order to overcome infidelity, it's important to gauge what the affair meant (or whether the pattern of one-night stands constitutes an addiction) and whether there is sincere remorse and responsibility taken for the deed. In addition, all extramarital activity must end, and the betrayer needs to make restitution and reparations. Without such, it's impossible for one party to find forgiveness. (Mind you, that's not forgetfulness, because many betrayed spouses cannot completely erase it from memory.) The offending party needs to deal attentively, with great empathy toward one's spouse and with frequent reassurance to resolve infidelity or the possibility of it in the future. Another way of summarizing this hurdle is to know why the infidelity occurred, have assurance it won't happen again, and state what consequences will occur if it does.

Marriages can recover from betrayal. Trust can be restored, for infidelity is often a wake-up call. Recovery will take a great deal of work, but if both parties are willing, the indiscretion can lead to greater ground as a married couple.

Accepting Divorce

Some marriages can't be fixed. Mine was one of them. For a short while, I hoped we would get back together, but there were multiple issues fraught with broken trust and what I saw as a pattern of fight or flight. At the first meeting with our attorneys, I broke down in tears as I came to terms with all of this. That was the day I knew my marriage was 100 percent over. In fact, I ran home to rewrite my will and do the rest of my husband's packing for him. I'd had it.

Even then, it was hard to accept the demise of our union, sealed in the college chapel, which had brought forth two beautiful boys. There are still sentimental times, but not because I want him back. Indeed, most women admit they can't fathom ever being intimate with their ex-husband again, even if the world's population depended on it! My sentiment stems from the broken dreams—the vacations never taken, the holidays never had, the school events never attended together with pride. It comes from what could have been, instead of what I truly had.

REAL AND IMAGINED LOSSES

Managing the memories and the necessary losses will surely tug at your heart, too. But when I'd start the wistful thinking, my friends would quickly step in, reminding me that I felt safer, healthier, and happier without him. One male friend, hearing that my husband asked to move back, implored, "Listen to what you're saying. If he wants the garage remote, the security code, and access to the boys, those are conveniences. Not a marriage." My friend was right.

Just as time helps reconciling couples, it also helps those divorcing. You must travel through the pain, not around it, to get to the other side. Don't worry about the marriage, and certainly not about your soon-to-be-former spouse. As mothers, we're supposed to figure out our children—when they need to go to the toilet, when they are hungry, when they need sleep, etc. But as wives and ex-wives, we're *not* our partner's mother. Your ex-husband must be responsible for himself and his future. If his poor choices impact his relationship with the children, then let him make or break that relationship of his own accord. Pick your battles wisely, and only where the children's welfare matters. Otherwise, stay out of his life, his decisions, and his future.

THE BLAME GAME

While it takes two parties to dance, one partner can really miss the beat. Only you know the energy and commitment you contributed to your marriage, but my guess is you did the very best you could at the time. There is absolutely no sense beating yourself up over past mistakes—yours, his, your children's, or even your extended family member's mistakes.

In fact, thinking about your marital missteps can become obsessive and lead you into deeper distress and depression. Your life is a continuum, and your marriage was only a stop. Try as best you can to focus on the future, to reframe things in a positive light. Much of the time, what you think determines how you feel. Quit asking "why me?" or "what could I have done?" Ruminating over this loss will keep you shackled by it.

If you're feeling continually lost without the framework of your marriage, it's time to seek professional help, and perhaps to begin something of your own (such as a new job or a new academic program) to force a refocus. Remember: You are your greatest gift to your own happiness and successful future.

Learning to Be Single

One woman I spoke with articulated the common feeling of socially not fitting in anywhere. Used to moving in a circle of couples, you might feel as if you're wearing a neon sign, hesitant to reveal your circumstances or making up excuses why you can't join others. Sooner or later, however, you'll want and need to venture out. Believe it or not, you don't need a man by your side to do so.

A friend described this as the "putting yourself back together" phase, a time when you make new friendships, begin new traditions, and even decide you might like some time to yourself.

"I revel in having the house to myself," another woman told me. And that is so true after you've shared living space with another adult. You can eat potato chips and sip iced tea for dinner, at midnight if you want. You can invite the dog or cat into the queen-sized bed, or like me, you can watch CNN in the middle of the night!

Indeed, it's perfectly fine to go it alone, for a while or forever. But the word *alone* does not mean a life destined to complete solitude. "Remember, you may be on your own, but you don't have to be alone," write Keith Anderson, M.D., and Roy MacSkimming in *On Your Own Again.* They stress that quality friendships are vital; friends act as mirrors that help us see ourselves.

Admittedly, some women have a larger appetite for solitude than others. There are women who can't take themselves to a restaurant with a good book, or attend a social function without a date. I'll admit it's different being single, and some events are easier than others. I'm glad I've pushed myself a little. I attend my neighborhood Christmas party even if I don't have a date. I go to church and graduation parties unaccompanied at times. And the thought of having a king-sized bed to myself in a wonderful hotel is a luxury, not a lament.

I can do these things because I've learned to treat myself well. I've seen some women postpone their dreams because they figure Prince Charming is on his way. There may well be a gentleman who will capture your heart and render you silly. But why wait? Create your own future, even if it's uncomfortable for the moment. Who ever said growth and change were easy?

One simple way to navigate the world independently is to do it with a friend. A girlfriend, a relative, even a platonic guy friend can accompany you when the thought of going solo is too troublesome. If you and a friend agree to have dinner, force yourself to take two cars, arriving alone and having a few moments to yourself. Each time you venture out, take gradual steps at social independence.

The same holds true for vacations. I'd traveled solo for business, but there were other small victories I had to create. I'd never rented a car on my own. I'd never single-parented a vacation nor explored different parts of the country completely solo, but I did those things too.

If you're still leery of setting out solo, look at it this way. We unattached women combat the perception enough that we're supposedly missing out on life. However, women often outlive men. Face the fact that you will be on your own for a few years regardless of your present circumstances. Would you rather learn to be independent now when you're younger and relatively active? Or would you rather wait until you need assistance in a wheelchair? I think you'll enjoy it now, and later too. My point: Be happy now. Embrace the opportunities before you.

A Great Escape

At some juncture during your separation, you or one of your children will likely remark, "Let's get out of here!" Indeed, little escapes with new scenery allow you to recharge and see yourself as a work in progress.

But where? That's the dilemma for many single parents accustomed to vacationing with an extra set of hands, not to mention the added income a dual-career family often lends to the effort. Rest assured, you do have options for a vacation. It's essential to your own mental health and to your children's sense of normalcy.

Sure, funds might be tighter. If that's the case, take those out-of-town friends up on their offer to visit. Do you know anyone in a fun city your kids haven't visited? Is there another family you could pool costs with, driving to a destination or renting accommodations? Have you accumulated frequent flier miles (or have relatives)? Join an alumni tour, a church outing, or some other singles group. Use caution as you would any time you travel, but don't allow your single status to keep you from exploring the globe.

Another alternative is to combine a business trip with an extended stay. Sure, it might mean having child care or asking another adult to accompany you to watch the kids while you attend meetings. But if you are going someplace fun with your expenses covered (and if an adult relative is willing to pick up her tab), this makes a lot of sense. I've been fortunate in that my writing involves the occasional travel feature. Because of assignments, I've included the boys on trips to Williamsburg, New England, and even on two sailings of the Disney Cruise Line.

Speaking of Disney, this seems to be most children's fantasy vacation. While I would not call this an inexpensive trip, it is possible to trim the costs of doing Walt Disney World. For starters, you can choose to stay at one of their value resorts on the property for under $100 per night, or choose to stay off-site at a budget-priced motel. (Though resort guests use Disney transportation free of charge.) While seeing everything would require a two-week stay, decide which parks are most important and stay fewer days. Plan your arrival early one morning and your departure late at night if you are flying. This eliminates another night's lodging. Bring snacks and eat at food-court restaurants rather than sit-down venues. Two small children might split a children's meal, if the portions are plentiful. Purchase Disney trinkets at home (such as autograph books, clothing, and the like) when you spot these on sale. Stash them in your suitcase to present as alternatives to pricey merchandise.

Finally, if you do crave that great escape on your own (sans children), read *Traveling Solo* by Eleanor Berman for advice and ideas on all sorts of vacations.

Dare to Date Again

I'm sure you've heard the cliché "once burned, twice cautious." Nowhere does that apply more than dating again after a failed, perhaps hurtful, relationship. Of course, there is no law that says you must date. In fact, entering into this arena too fast guarantees that you'll fall into a rebound relationship, which will lead you down another path of misery. If you require time to heal, you won't be in a better position to do so after surrendering time and energy to someone else. Or as someone so cleverly put it, "Why would you want someone else's butthead if you already had one?"

In time, most women who divorce will yearn for companionship, and if you focus on that factor, you're much better off than looking for Mr. Right or even Mr. Right For Now. Your goal should be to meet people. Period. This is a challenge if you had an active social life full of couple activities. But dating doesn't have to be all that daunting, with the right approach. Be thankful at this stage in your life that you know more of what you want, and that you realize what you have to offer another person. These assets far outweigh any re-entry fears.

SPOTTING OTHER SINGLES

So where do you find available men? Sure, clubs or bars are obvious choices, but if you're like me, you'd prefer an atmosphere of more substance. Look at outings with other single parents, classes at community colleges, religious or volunteer activities, or chance meetings at your favorite hangouts like bookstores or bowling alleys. You may form new friendships at professional meetings or parties hosted by friends. There are singles groups and volunteer associations designed to foster introductions. Some are free to join; others charge a fee to match you with compatible partners. Of course, the safest dates are those you know through friends who can vouch for character. Even men you meet at work might mask what they don't want you to see, and Lord knows how many men on the Internet can disguise their marital status for a cheap cyberthrill. There is a calculated risk in any dating. But I met a sane, safe man that way. You might too! I'd also advise against dating any married man, including a recently separated man who uses lines like "my wife didn't understand me." These guys, desperate to reattach, should use their energy to heal, grow, spend time with their children, and figure out what went wrong in their marriages *before* getting involved with another woman.

When you do venture out to meet someone in person, remember that you're expanding your horizon of contacts, and if you're lucky, you'll find a friend. Lower your sights a little. I'm not suggesting that you dump your standards. There's no sense dating a smoker if you know it's an immediate turn off to you. Besides, there isn't a National Jerk Registry to alert us women to mamma's boys, men who grope and paw, and men who wear gold rings when they're not with you! Therefore, our standards and intuition play important roles. Still, if you set your sights too high, aiming for perfection, you'll have many lonely Saturday nights. Give a little and you just might get a lot in return. I never pictured myself dating a man several years my senior. But was I in for a pleasant surprise! When presented with maturity, how refreshing and wonderful it was. This is what I mean about giving things a chance.

First Date Jitters

Adjusting your attitude and expectations calms the jitters. Refuse to obsess about what you'll wear, what your date will think, or any other aspect of this first meeting, for that's all it is—maybe a cup of coffee and some conversation.

The art of revealing your personality is gradual, both for you and the other person. If you try to impress, you'll surely fail. Thus, put yourself in your date's place. Doing so keeps you from wondering how you're coming across. He's feeling anxious too. He wants to make an equally good impression.

Meet at a neutral, public location where you have driven yourself. This is for safety and sanity's sake. If you find that the date is a disaster, you can politely cut it short. It's also a safe bet to stick with subjects like work and recreational interests as opposed to personal inadequacies or failings in a marriage. You don't want to seem as though you're sizing up your date. Similarly, too much unloading comes across as bitterness. We all have the proverbial baggage, but we don't necessarily need to advertise that fact.

Discuss things with kindness and compassion, and maintain good eye contact when listening and speaking. This means you're focusing on the other person, which is always flattering. Also, consider each other's expectations. As a guy friend confided, women tend to like a guy first, then find him attractive. Men, being more visually inclined, are physically attracted to women first. Then they fall in love.

NEXT STEPS

If you're fortunate enough to form a connection and a friendship, you'll wonder where this new relationship might lead. The majority of divorced women do remarry, in time, but that doesn't mean you must rush into a new union. You want to make sure this is the right move, and the only way you'll know is to proceed a bit cautiously.

As Dr. James C. Dobson has written, "Remember that respect precedes love. Build it stone upon stone." That's why it's wise to postpone sexual relations as long as possible. When the endorphins are raging is not the time to size up your relationship. Indeed, those love hormones will mask all the red flags and warning signs that this might *not* be the man for your future.

Additionally, know that what you see is indeed what you get. If you think you care for this man, but hope your love will change this habit or that peccadillo, think again.

Also, realize that every relationship is tested in due course. There's a natural pulling-back process that each of us does when we feel things getting too serious. John Gray often says men are like rubber bands—they stretch before springing back. We might do this because we are scared. It could be we feel our independence threatened. Or, for many men, it's the fear that we women will indeed want to change them. Again, part of the excitement of dating and falling in love later in life is the journey of exploration.

If your efforts are successful and the relationship is meant to be, you'll be well on your way to that one very satisfying moment. No, I'm not talking about sex. I'm not even talking about walking down the aisle. It's the moment when you revel in sheer delight as your former mate meets your current love. I believe it was Ivana Trump who claimed living well is the best revenge.

How Do I Know?

I purposely didn't call this section "How to Spot Mr. Right" because I want it to help women make the important decision of whether to stick with their marriage or form a new relationship with a future partner. Hopefully, this list will incite some answers, though all questions may not apply to each scenario:

- Can you be yourself with the man in your life?
- Are you treated well or mistreated in some way?
- Do you feel safe, both physically and emotionally, in this relationship?
- Is there absolute trust or do you feel pieces of the puzzle are missing?
- Do you feel a sense of support (that is, not usurping your authority but complementing it) in your parenting efforts?
- Can the two of you fight fairly? Or do disagreements never get negotiated?
- Do you still wonder if you could click with other men? Mere curiosity is a red flag that you might not be as grounded as you should be in this relationship.
- Does your husband respect you? Experts say that when the respect goes, the marriage is pretty much over.

- Does your man of the moment have female chums? Most women don't form platonic friendships with jerks. Besides, men learn valuable insights about us from spending time with other women.
- Is the man you're dating separated? If so, are you enabling him to flee rather than work on his marriage and keep the commitment to his family?
- Are you frequently reminded that you're thought of and loved?
- Is staying in this marriage a worse fear than venturing out on your own?

Onward Bound

You'll know you're healing from your marital separation when you feel calmer and better able to focus on the tasks of work, daily living, and parenting. You'll recognize a pattern of wellness that is reflected in your ideal weight, a good night's sleep, and a more pleasant demeanor. You'll smile. You'll laugh. No, not all the time, but you won't wake up every day consumed by feelings of change, loss, or panic. In essence, you'll be back to being your own best friend—with less angst, self-criticism, and blame.

New friends, new goals, new attitudes will take hold in your soul, and others will notice the shift in your life. In fact, I'll end with this little recollection from my own separation. It was merely weeks since my husband had walked out when I found myself in a parent-teacher conference, feeling wounded, overwhelmed, and distraught. I imagine I looked just the way I felt, and what an embarrassing moment that was.

Cut to two years later. I was still separated, but not yet divorced. One of the teachers I'd met with during that initial conference spotted me in the school hallway. She'd always struck me as being a little on the quiet side, so I expected she'd smile and keep walking. Our eyes met, and this time I held my head a lot higher than I did during that initial conference. To my surprise, she stopped me that day.

"You look great," she said with a broad smile. In that instant, I felt proud, no longer embarrassed. Everyone goes through tough times, I thought. We don't relish when others see us at our low points, but when we perk back up again, what a wonderful feeling that is!

Afterword

Shortly after my divorce was settled, a friend sent me some encouraging e-mail. At the time, the book you're about to finish was merely a dream, so you'll see how prescient his take truly was.

"I'm glad it's over for you, or at least this round is over," he said. "You survived. You will survive worse. Now you will help others survive as well. Even more so, you will be wiser for having gone through all of this."

Oh, I most assuredly do feel wiser, and fortunately a lot less weary than I did through those initial days and months of my marital separation. This book has helped put closure to that stage in my life, and I can only hope it's made some difference for you as well.

To end, I'd like to summarize the top ten things I've learned while researching this project and walking the path of separation and divorce:

- Never assume your friend's, sister's, or neighbor's marriage is perfect, for there very well could be cracks you don't see.
- Many among the married ranks don't realize what a safe harbor a warm, loyal spouse can be until it's way too late.
- It's better to be alone, relying upon good friends for communication and validation, than miserable in a silent union that wears you down.
- No woman should live with fear and intimidation. Ever.
- Helping children through adolescence is plenty. Navigating it for a husband is hopeless.
- Single parenting isn't a picnic, but the bond you form sticking with your children is irreplaceable.
- Yes, some dates can be disasters, but flirting and meeting potential partners is fun. And believe it or not, men and monogamy can co-exist in the same sentence. Who would have thought?
- The men who left their wives—for whatever reason or whatever person—often did them the biggest favor of their lives. Most of us women are stronger and more resourceful than we ever imagined.
- If you work hard, live right, and trust in God, there will be opportunities for you.
- The future is so much more pleasant to ponder than the past.

Resource Appendix

The following resources were useful me to during my own separation and divorce, and throughout the research of this book. I hope you'll find them helpful to you as well. – LHO

Chapter One: Suddenly Separated

Mister Rogers Talks With Parents by Fred M. Rogers and Barry Head (1983, Family Communications: Pittsburgh, Pa.)

Chapter Two: Looking after You

The Dance of Anger by Harriet G. Lerner, Ph.D. (1985, Harper & Row)

Healing an Angry Heart: Finding Solace in a Hostile World by Cardwell C. Nuckols, Ph.D. and Bill Chickering (1998, Health Communications)

Worry: Controlling It and Using It Wisely by Edward M. Hallowell, M.D. (1997, Pantheon Books)

Simple Abundance Journal of Gratitude by Sarah Ban Breathnach (1996, Warner Books)

How Could You Do That? The Abdication of Character, Courage and Conscience by Dr. Laura Schlessinger (1996, Harper Collins)

Shattered Faith: A Woman's Struggle to Stop the Catholic Church From Annulling Her Marriage by Sheila Rauch Kennedy (1998, Henry Holt)

In the Meantime: Finding Yourself and the Love You Want by Iyanla Vanzant (1998, Simon & Schuster)

Dr. Nancy Snyderman's Guide to Good Health by Nancy L. Snyderman, M.D. and Margaret Blackstone (1996, William Morrow & Co.)

Joan Lunden's Healthy Living by Joan Lunden and Laura Morton (1997, Crown Publishing)

American Medical Association's Complete Guide to Women's Health (1996, Random House)

Our Bodies, Ourselves for the New Century by Boston Women's Health Book Collective (1998, Touchstone Books)

Strong Women Stay Slim by Miriam E. Nelson, Ph.D. with Sarah Wernick, Ph.D. (1998, Bantam Books)

52 Relaxing Rituals and *52 Ways to Mend a Broken Heart* by Lynn Gordon (1996, Chronicle Books)

In Sickness and in Health by Mary E. O'Brien, M.D. (1991, Health Press)

Living with the Passive-Aggressive Man by Scott Wetzler, Ph.D.

Dating For Dummies by Dr. Joy Browne (1997, IDG Books)

For Yourself: The Fulfillment of Female Sexuality by Lonnie Garfield Barbach (1991, New American Library)

Sex For One: The Joy of Self-loving by Betty Dodson (1996, Crown Publishing)

Chapter Three: Coping with Your Children

Second Chances: Men, Women and Children a Decade After Divorce by Judith Wallerstein and Sandra Blakeslee (1996, Houghton Mifflin)

Helping Your Kids Cope with Divorce the Sandcastles Way by M. Gary Neuman with Patricia Romanowski (1998, Times Books)

Vicky Lansky's Divorce Book for Parents by Vicky Lansky (1996, Book Peddlers)

Surviving The Breakup: How Children and Parents Cope with Divorce by Judith S. Wallerstein and Joan Berlin Kelly (1980, BasicBooks)

The Angry Child by Timothy F. Murphy, Ph.D. and Loriann Hoff Oberlin (2000, Clarkson Potter/Crown Publishing)

Mom's House, Dad's House: A Complete Guide for Parents Who Are Separated, Divorced or Remarried by Isolina Ricci, Ph.D. (1997, Fireside)

"Does Wednesday Mean Mom's House or Dad's?" Parenting Together While Living Apart by Marc J. Ackerman, Ph.D. (1997, Wiley)

The Wounded Male by Steven Farmer (1991, Ballantine Books)

Angry Men, Passive Men by Marvin Allen with Jo Robinson (1993, Fawcett Columbine)

Dealing with Difficult Men by Judith Segal, Ph.D. (1993, Lowell House)

Mom, Can I Have That and *Dr. Tightwad's Money-Smart Kids* by Janet Bodnar (1996 and 1997, Kiplinger Books)

Giving The Love That Heals: A Guide for Parents by Harville Hendrix, Ph.D. and Helen Hunt (1997, Pocket Books)

The Complete Single Mother: Reassuring Answers to Your Most Challenging Concerns by Andrea Engber and Leah Klungness, Ph.D.

The Parental Alienation Syndrome by Richard A. Gardner, M.D. (1998, Creative Therapeutics)

Helping Your Child Through Your Divorce by Florence Bienenfeld, Ph.D. (1995, Hunter House)

- The National Association for the Education of Young Children (NAEYC) 1-800-424-2460
- Child Care Aware 1-800-424-2246
- "Talking With Families About Divorce" a booklet, published by Fred Rogers & Family Communications (send a self-addressed, stamped, business-size envelope to Family Communications, Inc., 4802 Fifth Avenue, Pittsburgh, PA 15213 or call 412-687-2990)

Resources for Children

A Separation in My Family by Wendy Deaton (1994, Hunter House)

Let's Talk About It: Divorce by Fred Rogers (1996, Philomel Books)

Chapter Four: Navigating the Legal Landscape

Money-Smart Divorce: What Women Need To Know About Money and Divorce by Esther M. Berger, CFP (1996, Simon & Schuster)

Divorce: A Woman's Guide to Getting a Fair Share by Patricia Phillips, J.D. (1995, IDG Books)

Divorce & Money: How to Make the Best Financial Decisions During Divorce by Violet Woodhouse, CFP and Victoria Collins, Ph.D. with M.C. Blakeman (1998, Nolo)

What Every Woman Should Know About Divorce and Custody by Gayle Rosenwald Smith, J.D. and Sally Abrahms (1998, Perigee)

How To File Your Own Divorce by Edward A. Haman (1997, Sourcebooks)

The New Creative Divorce by Mel Krantzler, Ph.D. and Pat Krantzler, M.A. (1998, Adams Media Corporation)

Healthy Divorce by Craig Everett and Sandra Volgy Everett (1998, Jossey-Bass)

Working at Home While The Kids Are There, Too by Loriann Hoff Oberlin (1997, Career Press)

Divorce For Dummies by John Ventura and Mary Reed (1998, IDG Books)

How to Write Your Own Premarital Agreement by Edward A. Haman (1998, Sourcebooks)

The American Academy of Matrimonial Lawyers, Chicago, IL 312-263-6477

Chapter Five: Preserving Your Personal Safety

The Battered Woman by Lenore Walker (1980, Harper Collins)

What To Do When Love Turns Violent by Marian Betancourt (1997, Harper Perennial)

You Can Be Free by Ginny NiCarthy and Sue Davidson (1997, Seal Press)

Getting Free by Ginny NiCarthy, M.S.W. (1997, Seal Press)

Before It's Too Late by Robert J. Ackerman, Ph.D. with Susan E. Pickering (1995, Health Communications)

The Verbally Abusive Relationship and *Verbal Abuse Survivors Speak Out* by Patricia Evans (1996 (revised) and 1993, Adams Media Corporation)

End The Pain by Lynn Hawker, Ph.D. and Terry Bicehouse (1995, Zinn Communications)

Stop Domestic Violence by Lou Brown, Francois Dubau, and Merritt McKeon, J.D. (1997, St. Martin's Griffin)

When Men Batter Women by Neil Jacobson, Ph.D. and John Gottman, Ph.D. (1998, Simon & Schuster)

The Abusive Personality by Donald G. Dutton, Ph.D. (1998, The Guilford Press)

The Batterer: A Psychological Profile by Donald G. Dutton, Ph.D. with Susan K. Golant (1995, BasicBooks)

When Violence Begins At Home by K. J. Wilson, Ed.D. (1997, Hunter House)

A Woman's Guide to Personal Safety by Janeé Harteau and Holly Keegel (1998, Fairview Press)

Not An Easy Target: Paxton Quigley's Self-Protection for Women by Paxton Quigley (1995, Fireside)

National Domestic Violence Hotline 1-800-799-SAFE (7233)

Resources for Children

Mommy and Daddy Are Fighting by Susan Paris and Illustrated by Gail Labinski (1986, Seal Press)

Chapter Six: Your Financial Future

Simplify Your Christmas by Elaine St. James (1998, Andrews McMeel)

No-Load Stocks by Charles B. Carlson, CFA (1997, NorthStar Financial, Inc.)

Writing For Money by Loriann Hoff Oberlin (1994, Writer's Digest Books)

Working at Home While The Kids Are There, Too by Loriann Hoff Oberlin (1997, Career Press)

The College Costs and Financial Aid Handbook (1999, College Entrance Examination Board)

Financing Graduate School by Patricia McWade (1996, Peterson's Guides)

Every Woman's Guide To Financial Security by Ann Z. Peterson and Stephen M. Rosenberg, CFP (1997, Career Press)

The 9 Steps To Financial Freedom and *The Courage To Be Rich* by Suze Orman (1997, Crown and 1999, Riverhead Books)

Wealth On Minimal Wage by James Streamer (1998, Berkley Publishing Group)

The Wealthy Barber by David Chilton (1998, Prima)

Never Balance Your Checkbook On Tuesday by Nancy Dunnan (1997, Harper Collins)

Suddenly Single: Money Skills for Divorcées and Widows by Kerry Hannon (1998, Wiley)

Making The Most Of Your Money by Jane Bryant Quinn (1997, Simon & Schuster)

Ernst & Young's Financial Planning For Women (1999, Wiley)

Prince Charming Isn't Coming by Barbara Stanny (1999, Penguin)

Investing on a Shoestring by Barbara O'Neill (1999, Dearborn Publishing)

The Wall Street Journal Guide To Understanding Personal Finance (series also includes *Money & Investing* and *Planning Your Financial Future*)

- "What You Should Know About Financial Planning" booklet from Certified Financial Planner Board of Standards 1-888-237-6275.
- "Social Security: What Every Woman Should Know" contact your local social security office
  Energy Savers booklet
  P.O. Box 3048 — Dept. P
  Merrifield, VA 22116 1-800-363-3732
- Association for Children for Enforcement of Support (ACES)
  Toledo, Ohio 1-800-537-7072
- National Foundation for Consumer Credit
  1-800-284-1723
- U.S. Department of Education
  1-800-433-3243

Chapter Seven: Carving Out a Career

What Color Is Your Parachute? by Richard Nelson Bolles (1999, Prima)

Financing Graduate School by Patricia McWade (1996, Peterson's Guides)

Working at Home While The Kids Are There, Too by Loriann Hoff Oberlin (1997, Career Press)

Cool Careers For Dummies by Marty Nemko and Paul and Sarah Edwards (1998, IDG Books)

101 Ways To Power Up Your Job Search by J. Thomas Buck, William R. Matthews, and Robert N. Leech (1997, McGraw Hill)

The Job Bank Guide To Employment Services (1999, Adams Media Corporation)

The Temp Track by Peggy O'Connell Justice (1994, Peterson's Guides)

The Resumé Catalog: 200 Damn Good Examples by Yana Parker (1996, Ten Speed Press)

Resumés That Knock 'Em Dead, Cover Letters That Knock 'Em Dead, and *Knock 'Em Dead 1999* by Martin J. Yate (1997 and 1999, Adams Media Corporation)

200 Letters For Job Hunters by William S. Frank (1993, Ten Speed Press)

The Unofficial Guide To Acing The Interview by Michelle Tullier (1999, IDG Books)

101 Great Answers To The Toughest Interview Questions by Ron Fry (1996, Career Press)

101 Great Answers To The Toughest Job Search Problems by Ollie Stevenson (1995, Career Press)

Networking Skills That Will Get You the Job You Want by Cherie Kerr (1999, Betterway Books)

Not Guilty! The Good News About Working Mothers by Betty Holcomb (1998, Scribner)

Chapter Eight: Household Hints and Car Care

Lucille's Car Care by Lucille Treganowan with Gina Catanzarite (1996, Hyperion)

Household Hints & Handy Tips published by Reader's Digest (1995, Reader's Digest)

Great Health Hints & Handy Tips published by Reader's Digest (1994, Reader's Digest)

New Complete Do-It-Yourself Manual by Reader's Digest (1991, Reader's Digest)

Everyday Home Repairs (1988, Black and Decker Home Improvement Library)

The Home Repair Emergency Handbook by Gene Schnaser (1992, Galahad Books)

1000 Questions About Home Repair & Maintenance by Al Carrell (1997, Summit Publishing Group)

The Consumer Bible by Mark Green (1998, Workman)

The Everything Home Improvement Book by Tom Philbin (1997, Adams Media Corporation)

Better Homes & Gardens New Garden Book (1990, Meredith Corporation)

National Highway Traffic Safety Administration
Booklet on buying a safer car
1-800-424-9393

Handy Ma'am by Beverly DeJulio (1999, Dearborn Publishing)

Chapter Nine: Learning to Lighten Up

The Angry Child by Timothy F. Murphy, Ph.D. and Loriann Hoff Oberlin (2000, Clarkson Potter/Crown Publishing)

Anatomy of an Illness by Norman Cousins (1991, Bantam Doubleday Dell)

How To Make Luck: Seven Secrets Lucky People Use To Succeed by Marc Meyers (1999, Renaissance Books)

A Bend In The Road Is Not The End Of The Road by Joan Lunden and Andrea Cagan (1998, William Morrow)

In the Meantime: Finding Yourself and the Love You Want by Iyanla Vanzant (1998, Simon & Schuster)

Opening Up: The Healing Power of Expressing Emotions by James W. Pennebaker, Ph.D. (1990, The Guilford Press)

Untying the Knot by Deborah Brodie and Ashton Applewhite (1999, Griffin)

The Joy of Being Single, 101 Reasons Why a Cat Is Better Than a Man and *101 More Reasons Why a Cat Is Better Than a Man* by Allia Zobel (1992 and 1994 and 1997, Adams Media Corporation)

How Are Men Like Noodles by Cindy Garner (1995, Andrews McMeel)

How to Make Your Man Behave in 21 Days Or Less, Using the Secrets of Professional Dog Trainers by Karen Salmansohn (1994, Workman)

101 Uses for an Ex-Husband by Richard Smith (1997, Warner Books)

America's Dumbest Dates by Merry Bloch Jones (1999, Andrews McMeel)

Women Are from Venus, Men Are from Hell by Amanda Newman (1999, Adams Media Corporation)

Chapter Ten: Exploring New Horizons

Getting Back Together by Bettie Youngs Bilicki, Ph.D. and Masa Goetz, Ph.D. (1990, Adams Media Corporation)

Surviving Infidelity by Rona Subotnik, M.F.C.C. and Gloria G. Harris, Ph.D. (1999, Adams Media Corporation)

Betrayed: How You Can Restore Sexual Trust and Rebuild Your Life by Riki Robbins, Ph.D. (1998, Adams Media Corporation)

Infidelity: A Survival Guide by Don-David Lusterman, Ph.D. (1998, New Harbinger)

Private Lies: Infidelity and the Betrayal of Intimacy by Frank Pittman (1990, W.W. Norton & Co.)

Surviving An Affair by Dr. Williard F. Harley, Jr. and Dr. Jennifer Harley Chalmers (1998, Revell)

Fighting For Your Marriage by Howard Markman, Scott Stanley, Susan L. Blumberg, and Dean S. Edell (1996, Jossey-Bass)

On Your Own Again by Keith Anderson, M.D. and Roy MacSkimming (1998, McClelland & Stewart)

You Can Get Over Divorce by Pat Hudson, Ph.D. (1998, Prima)

365 Reflections On Being Single by Dahlia Porter (1999, Adams Media Corporation)

Flying Solo: Single Women in Midlife by Carol Anderson, Ph.D., Susan Stewart, and Sona Dimidjian (1995, W.W. Norton & Co.)

Being Single In A Couple's World by Xavier Amador, Ph.D. and Judith Kiersky, Ph.D. (1998, Simon & Schuster)

Cutting Loose: Why Women Who End Their Marriages Do So Well by Ashton Applewhite (1997, Harper Collins)

How To Mend A Broken Heart: Letting Go and Moving On by Aleta Koman, M.Ed. (1997, NTC/Contemporary Books)

Traveling Solo by Eleanor Berman (1999, Globe Pequot)

It's a Guy Thing: An Owner's Manual for Women by David Deida (1997, Health Communications)

When In Doubt Check Him Out by Joseph J. Culligan (1996, Hallmark Press)

Romantic Deception, Six Signs He's Lying by Dr. Sally Caldwell, (1999, Adams Media Corporation)

Six Keys To Creating The Life You Desire by Mitch Meyerson and Laurie Ashner (1999, New Harbinger)

Dating For Dummies by Dr. Joy Browne (1997, IDG Books)

The Complete Idiot's Guide to Dating by Dr. Judy Kuriansky (1999, Alpha Books)

The Unofficial Guide to Dating Again by Tina Tessina, Ph.D. (1998, Macmillan)

Mars And Venus On a Date and *Mars And Venus Starting Over* by John Gray, Ph.D. (1997 and 1998, Harper Collins)

The Seven Dumbest Relationship Mistakes Smart People Make by Carolyn Bushong (1997, Villard)

Are You The One For Me? by Barbara DeAngelis, Ph.D. (1992, Bantam Doubleday Dell)

Living In A Step Family Without Getting Stepped On by Kevin Leman, Ph.D. (1994, Thomas Nelson)

Index

B

C

D

E

F

G

H

I

T

U

V

W

Y

About the Author

Loriann Hoff Oberlin is the author of *Writing For Money* (Writer's Digest Books) and *Working at Home While The Kids Are There, Too* (Career Press). Ms. Oberlin has served as co-author on *The Insider's Guide To Pittsburgh* (Falcon Publishing), and teamed with Timothy F. Murphy, Ph.D., a psychologist and Pennsylvania State Senator, to write *The Angry Child* (Clarkson Potter/Crown Publishing).

Ms. Oberlin has written a monthly column on work and family for the *Pittsburgh Business Times*, and contributes to national magazines. When not working on books or articles, she teaches writing workshops and lectures at conferences around the country. Ms. Oberlin has two young sons.